Intensive English Programs in Postsecondary Settings

Edited by Nicholas Dimmitt and
Maria Dantas-Whitney

Case Studies in TESOL Practice Series

Jill Burton, Series Editor

Teachers of English to Speakers of Other Languages, Inc.

Typeset in Berkeley and Belwe
by Capitol Communications Systems, Inc., Crofton, Maryland USA
Printed by Kirby Lithographic Company, Inc. USA
Indexed by Coughlin Indexing Services, Annapolis, Maryland USA

Teachers of English to Speakers of Other Languages, Inc.
700 South Washington Street, Suite 200
Alexandria, Virginia 22314 USA
Tel 703-836-0774 • Fax 703-836-6447 • E-mail tesol@tesol.org • http://www.tesol.org/

Director of Communications and Marketing: Helen Kornblum
Managing Editor: Marilyn Kupetz
Additional Reader: Marcia Annis
Cover Design: Capitol Communications Systems, Inc.

ISBN 0-939791-96-X
Library of Congress Control No. 2001 132415

Dedication

For John, Thomas, and Philip, my constant sources of support and inspiration.

Maria Dantas-Whitney

For Hongsuda and our son, Raymond, the love of both our lives, born during the making of this book.

Nicholas Dimmitt

Table of Contents

Acknowledgments

We are grateful to David Eskey for his early support of this project. We have benefited greatly from Jill Burton's wise and generous counsel; this book is much improved because of her insightful and patient mentoring. We also want to thank Marilyn Kupetz for her helpful and professional style of collaborating with us. Finally, we would like to thank our families, who supported us and encouraged us to finish this book.

Series Editor's Preface

The Case Studies in TESOL Practice series offers innovative and effective examples of practice from the point of view of the practitioner. The series brings together from around the world communities of practitioners who have reflected and written on particular aspects of their teaching. Each volume in the series will cover one specialized teaching focus.

◈ CASE STUDIES

Why a TESOL series focusing on case studies of teaching practice?

Much has been written about case studies and where they fit in a mainstream research tradition (e.g., Nunan, 1992; Stake, 1995; Yin, 1994). Perhaps more importantly, case studies also constitute a public recognition of the value of teachers' reflection on their practice and constitute a new form of teacher research—or teacher valuing. Case studies support teachers in valuing the uniqueness of their classes, learning from them, and showing how their experience and knowledge can be made accessible to other practitioners in simple but disciplined ways. They are particularly suited to practitioners who want to understand and solve teaching problems in their own contexts.

These case studies are written by practitioners who are able to portray real experience by providing detailed descriptions of teaching practice. These qualities invest the cases with teacher credibility, and make them convincing and professionally interesting. The cases also represent multiple views and offer immediate solutions, thus providing perspective on the issues and examples of useful approaches. Informative by nature, they can provide an initial database for further, sustained research. Accessible to wider audiences than many traditional research reports, however, case studies have democratic appeal.

◈ HOW THIS SERIES CAN BE USED

The case studies lend themselves to pre- and in-service teacher education. Because the context of each case is described in detail, it is easy for readers to compare the cases with and evaluate them against their own circumstances. To respond to the wide range of language environments in which TESOL functions, cases have been selected from EFL, ESL, and bilingual education settings around the world.

The 12 or so case studies in each volume are easy to follow. Teacher writers describe their teaching context and analyze its distinctive features: the particular demands of their context, the issues they have encountered, how they have effectively addressed the issues, what they have learned. Each case study also offers readers practical suggestions—developed from teaching experience—to adapt and apply to their own teaching.

Already in published or in preparation are volumes on

- academic writing programs
- action research
- assessment practices
- bilingual education
- community partnerships
- content-based language instruction
- distance learning
- English for specific purposes
- gender and TESOL
- grammar teaching in teacher education
- interaction and language learning
- international teaching assistants
- journal writing
- mainstreaming
- teacher education
- technology in the classroom
- teaching English as a foreign language in primary schools
- teaching English from a global perspective
- teaching English to the world

◈ THIS VOLUME

In this volume, authors explain how full-time English language programs are planned, taught, and managed in different parts of the world. The nature of intensive language programs—with their focused students, goals, and settings—are examined by teachers and course developers, who offer straightforward, practical information for the aspiring intensive language teacher and programmer while also revealing and evaluating their own creative solutions and experimental programs.

Jill Burton
University of South Australia, Adelaide

CHAPTER 1

Intensive English Instruction: Tales of Trials, Battles, and Accomplishments

Maria Dantas-Whitney and Nicholas Dimmitt

Intensive English programs (IEPs) have strived over the years to establish credibility and promote the kind of innovation that would be embraced by their administrative counterparts and collaborating institutions (Stoller & Christison, 1994). Since 1941, when the first U.S. IEP was established at the University of Michigan (Kaplan, 1997), IEPs have grown and developed into a sophisticated collection of programs and institutions throughout the world. Today IEPs are supported by professional associations such as Teachers of English to Speakers of Other Languages (TESOL) and Association of International Educators (originally NAFSA) and aided by organizations such as University and College Intensive English Programs (UCIEP) and The American Association of Intensive English Programs (AAIEP), which provide member programs with guidelines for professional standards and evaluation services as well as a forum for information exchange. Most recently, the creation of The Commission on English Language Program Accreditation (see *Commission on English Language Program Accreditation*, 2001) has represented another important step for the promotion of excellence and professionalism in IEPs.

All IEPs share the purpose of providing intensive English instruction to students at the postsecondary level (i.e., 18–30 hours per week), but program types vary widely within the United States and elsewhere. Many IEPs are affiliated with colleges or universities; others are independent. IEPs also differ in size, management structure, and instructional practice. Although most IEPs emphasize academic preparation, many programs welcome students who seek English study for professional or personal purposes. Within this wide variety of program types, IEPs have a common mission:

> to provide ESL training, using qualified professionals in a logical and developing sequence of courses to guide the students to a level of mastery of the English language that will lead to eventual success in a degree or certificate program (Staczek & Carkin, 1984, p. 294)

IEPs are what Eskey (1997) calls *nontraditional entities*. He explains that they may never become traditional programs because IEPs

- serve nontraditional student populations
- employ nontraditional faculty

- feature nontraditional curricula directed toward nontraditional academic objectives, and

- are usually locked into nontraditional administrative and budgetary structures. (p. 21)

◈ STUDENTS

Most IEPs serve a heterogeneous group of students who often only have in common the goal of learning English in a relatively short period of time. In a typical IEP classroom, one can find students who come from different countries, who have diverse educational backgrounds, and who have a variety of purposes and motivations for studying English. As a rule, these students have not yet been admitted to degree programs, so the IEP serves as their so-called academic home. Thus, IEPs often provide a variety of support services that are not commonly offered by traditional academic units. Many IEPs coordinate orientation programs, social events, field trips, and other cultural opportunities (e.g., home stays and conversation partners) for students. In addition, IEP advisors play a major role in counseling students on personal, academic, and immigration concerns (e.g., dealing with culture shock, applying to degree programs, fulfilling visa requirements).

◈ FACULTY

In describing the absolute essentials of IEPs, Stoller (1994) suggests that "perhaps the truly inviolable core of an IEP is an interested, involved, and creative faculty" (p. 5), adding that "professionals who create a collaborative working environment with a continual interchange of ideas and who are granted the freedom to innovate are essential to an effective IEP" (p. 5). Indeed, because IEP instructors generally spend long hours in the classroom in direct contact with students, most of their professional concerns revolve around delivering a curriculum that is relevant to students' needs and challenges.

◈ CURRICULUM

Because program types are so varied and student purposes so diverse, IEP curricula typically address a wide range of competencies and skills. Most IEPs, however, offer a combination of courses that could be classified as English for general purposes (EGP) or English for academic purposes (EAP). Courses in EGP often involve instruction through cultural and general interest themes and activities that integrate the four language skills (reading, writing, listening, and speaking) in meaningful contexts. Collaborative and task-based communicative approaches are particularly suitable for these settings. These approaches are characterized by features described by Nunan (1991):

1. An emphasis on learning to communicate through interaction in the target language

2. The introduction of authentic texts into the learning situation

3. The provision of opportunities for learners to focus, not only on language, but also on the learning process itself

4. An enhancement of the learner's own personal experiences as important in contributing elements to classroom learning

5. An attempt to link classroom language learning with language activation outside the classroom. (p. 279)

EAP courses might also include the elements described above; however, they aim to simulate more closely the demands of classes in the different academic disciplines. In North American universities, EAP's content-based emphasis has evolved into several models for curriculum design, including (a) a theme-based approach, which organizes instructional materials and activities around academic content units; (b) a sheltered approach, which involves the teaching of a content class to a group of second language learners; and (c) an adjunct model, in which students attend two linked courses: a mainstream content class (i.e., with native speakers) and a language support class (Brinton, Snow, & Wesche, 1989; Snow & Brinton, 1997). The strength of EAP instruction is in its ability to address the specific demands of students' academic disciplines; however, Benesch (2001) reminds us that a critical stance is needed in EAP, one that enables students to "help shape academic goals and assignments rather than passively carrying them out" (p. xv).

As in all other language programs, issues related to assessment are also prevalent in IEPs. For programs preparing students to enter colleges and universities in the United States, the Test of English as a Foreign Language (TOEFL) has had a great impact on curricular and administrative policies. Many IEPs find themselves in a serious dilemma. On one hand, they try to provide students with the comprehensive academic preparation that is necessary to succeed in postsecondary educational settings. On the other hand, many U.S. colleges and universities only require a score on the TOEFL for admission, thus undermining the value of IEP course work. This incongruity has led many IEPs to work closely with university admissions offices to reformulate admissions criteria related to language proficiency. As a result, an increasing number of U.S. universities now accept an IEP's recommendation, based on a student's successful completion of its advanced levels, in lieu of a TOEFL score.

◈ ADMINISTRATION

Administrative structures also vary widely among IEPs, and directors and coordinators face special challenges related to the nontraditional nature and marginal status of their programs. IEPs based on college and university campuses often deal with oppressive budgetary arrangements and hierarchical structures that give administrators little decision-making power (Eskey, 1997). Independent IEPs, although granted more administrative freedom, cannot take advantage of campus-based facilities and services; this represents great challenges for student recruitment and retention. Christison and Stoller (1997) contend that effective IEP administrators must act in four major roles: as leaders, promoters, organizers, and visionaries. Each of these roles represents a complex range of "skills, knowledge and expertise," which are often learned "by trial and error" (p. vii).

◈ THIS VOLUME

Because their students, faculty, curricula and administration generally do not fit the conventional structures found in other academic programs, IEPs worldwide have had a shared history of struggle and quest for recognition. In this volume, we showcase IEPs that have engaged in battles and have become stronger and more effective as a result. The program models featured here were created out of a desire to find solutions for problems common to many. It is our hope that the chapters in this book will stimulate dialogue and provide inspiration for IEP teachers and administrators who face similar challenges.

Part 1: Developing Curricular Models

IEPs are for the most part self-supporting units offering noncredit classes. Although this structure offers countless disadvantages to students and faculty (e.g., budget fluctuations, staffing challenges, rising student/teacher ratios), it does provide flexibility in curricular change and innovation. It is usually possible for IEPs to experiment with new courses without having to go through university curriculum committees. This allows teachers to try out new ideas and teaching methods, and, as Stoller and Christison (1994) suggest, encourages professional development while avoiding burn out. "These efforts can boost faculty morale, revitalize faculty members, and bring valuable recognition to the program from outside" (p. 20).

Because of changing student populations and evolving curricula from various academic departments, it is crucial for IEPs to adapt instruction to fit different needs. IEPs that do not remain relevant with appropriate content and classes for students' and departmental needs will not be effective.

Chapters in this section represent curricular innovations that can be adapted to fit different program types. Smith-Palinkas, Tortorella, and Flaitz's discussion of their IEP's conversion of its discrete-skills curriculum into a combination content-integrated and skills-based curriculum exemplifies such innovations (chapter 2). The implications of such a curriculum change can be applied to numerous types of IEPs throughout the world. In chapter 3, Dantas-Whitney, Larson, and Dowling describe the comprehensive review and revision of their IEP's curriculum to create academic bridges to the university throughout the program materials and courses. This chapter addresses the need for programs to remain relevant and to search for ways to empower students for success in their post-IEP studies. Rilling (chapter 4) writes about the development of an advanced writing course for ESL graduate students using a genre-based approach tailored to the students' specific academic disciplines. This chapter represents another example of customizing curriculum to meet student needs. (For more information about L2 academic writing programs, see Leki, 2001.) All three chapters in this section present original curricular models useful to many IEPs.

Part 2: Creating Collaborative Partnerships

Because of the autonomous nature of IEPs, they must operate independently but in partnership with different units and agencies. Kaplan (1997) lists 24 possible IEP contacts. For IEPs located on a college or university campus, the challenge to ensure that their students share the same privileges as other students in degree-granting programs forces them to keep in close contact with campus housing, health services, computer and recreational facilities, and other student services. Campus-based IEPs also struggle with differing administrative configurations that produce partnerships with a variety of academic units (e.g., many IEPs are housed in academic departments such as English or linguistics; others are connected with continuing education, extension, or international programs).

In addition, many IEPs align themselves with graduate programs in TESOL, so a great deal of research goes on in IEPs, and new instructional practices are tried out. Reppen and Stoller (chapter 5) and Hind (chapter 6) describe efforts to forge stronger relationships between IEPs and MATESOL programs.

Partnerships with educational funding agencies and other educational institutions are also common. In chapter 7, Miller and Crandall write about a partnership between The Center for Applied Linguistics and the United States Agency for International Development (USAID) to create an innovative IEP model for Honduran students preparing for undergraduate work in the United States. Harrington, Jensen, and Rosen describe a partnership between an Australian University and a Korean University to establish a collaborative TEFL master's degree program in an IEP mode (chapter 8).

Part 3: Breaking New Ground

Because it was impossible to describe all ground-breaking contributions by IEPs over the years, we have chosen the chapters in this section to serve as exemplars of vision and determination by IEP teachers and administrators. These are case studies of battles with administrations and academic departments for credibility and recognition. The norm for IEPs is that courses be noncredit and not count toward graduation requirements. IEP teachers do not typically hold the same contractual status as other faculty, and IEP students often do not receive the same institutional support and assistance as local students. All of these factors contribute to the perception of IEPs as marginalized. These chapters show that with determination and perseverance, this perception can be changed. IEPs can overcome marginalization and break new ground in areas of professional development, student advocacy, and recognition of the importance of IEPs in academic organizations.

In chapter 9, Brooks writes about the pursuit of academic credit for IEP classes—a quest for legitimacy of a program. Chapter 10 presents Schwartz's impassioned description of her pursuit for university-level support for students with learning challenges, which entailed long-term advocacy for these students. Hoekje argues for the improvement of professional development and teacher evaluation practices in chapter 11.

◈ CONCLUSION

This volume reflects the change and development of IEPs in the TESOL world today. These chapters give insights into the struggles, accomplishments, and successful work being done in IEPs internationally. The future of IEPs is dependent on creative and dynamic teachers and administrators who continue to look for better and more effective ways to deliver the curriculum and courses that meet the needs of students and the requirements of academic stakeholders. We hope that this collection of case studies will contribute to the continued success of IEPs in your context and around the world.

◈ CONTRIBUTORS

Maria Dantas-Whitney is an instructor at the English Language Institute, Oregon State University, in the United States. She has held several administrative positions in program coordination and student advising. She has also served as president of Oregon TESOL and chair of TESOL's IEP interest section. Her main areas of research are collaborative learning, content-based instruction, self-directed learning, and critical reflection. She is currently working on a PhD in teacher education.

Nicholas Dimmitt is an assistant professor at the Asian Institute of Technology (AIT), in Thailand. For the past 6 years, he has collaborated in the development, administration, and teaching of AIT's pre-MA IEP students. He received his MA in TESOL from San Francisco State University, and his PhD in educational administration from the University of Southern California. He has been a teacher and teacher educator in IEPs at the University of Southern California, San Francisco State University, Oregon State University, the University of Bahrain, and the American University of Armenia.

PART 1

Developing Curricular Models

CHAPTER 2

"Cont-Int" Curriculum: A Content-Integrated-Skills-Based Approach

Barbara Smith-Palinkas, Donna M. Tortorella, and Jeffra Flaitz

◈ INTRODUCTION

When intensive English programs (IEPs) were first introduced to the United States in the 1970s, a theoretical shift was underway in the field of foreign and second language teaching. The conventional grammar-based, discrete-skills, "drill-and-kill" approach to language learning was beginning to give way to a methodology more oriented toward communication, fluency, meaning, and learner autonomy. At the same time, the whole language approach was gaining respect and popularity in education at large, and many professionals in the field began enthusiastically to explore the merits of content-based instruction (CBI), an approach that sought to embed language learning naturally into the learning of other subject matter.

Congruent with this new trend was a change in philosophy about the treatment of the language skills: listening, speaking, reading, writing, and "grammaring," the fifth skill proposed by Diane Larsen-Freeman (1999). The seamless relationship and interdependence among the five skills was highlighted throughout the professional literature, and the expression *integrated skills* replaced *discrete skills* as an organizing schema for curricula.

IEPs, though eager to implement the latest methods in teaching English to speakers of other languages (ESOL), nonetheless tended to shy away from adopting the integrated skills approach and CBI as curricular choices. Instead, CBI modules were unsystematically and sparingly integrated into programs that were basically dominated by an overall discrete skills curriculum. This was perhaps due to the imposing influence of the noninteractive, skills-oriented Test of English as a Foreign Language (TOEFL) on the clientele of university-based IEPs, on the one hand, and the urgency of bringing international students up to speed linguistically, on the other.

This chapter details the experience of one IEP that decided to take the leap—and the risk—of converting its discrete-skills curriculum into a quasi-integrated-skills, quasi-content-based hybrid. More accurately, the IEP adopted a "cont-int" curriculum, or one that is content-integrated and skills-based (CISB). That is to say, the program fully embraces neither CBI nor integrated skills instruction but has modified both to suit its particular needs and developments in the field.

A CISB curriculum, then, acknowledges the critical nature of the five skills, and they function as the basis of the IEP's pedagogical plan. It also recognizes the benefits of embedding language in meaningful contexts and providing opportunities for authentic interaction. Thus, the curriculum is not so much content based as it is content integrated and skills based. The main differences between a discrete-skills curriculum and a CISB curriculum are represented in Table 1.

A fuller description of the nature of this IEP follows, set within the organizational and functional framework of IEPs in general.

◈ CONTEXT

The English Language Institute (ELI) at the University of South Florida (USF) was founded in 1978, about the same time that many other IEPs came into being, and its birth coincided with the creation of an applied linguistics graduate track offered in conjunction with the existing theoretical linguistics track in the MA program. After more than 20 years in operation, it has prepared some 500 ESL teachers for the classroom, spawned numerous research studies, had a faculty that regularly publishes and presents at professional conferences, and provided teaching assistant-ships to some 15–20 graduate students every year.

The institute is directed by a tenured faculty member from the Division of Languages and Linguistics, the academic unit to which it is attached, and the program delivers English for academic purposes (EAP) to a population of approxi-mately 450 students annually, mostly U.S. university bound, from some 58 different countries. The institute offers three semester-length programs per year, 15 weeks during the fall and spring, and 13 weeks during the summer. Students in four levels are enrolled in five classes that meet for a total of 25 hours per week.

The ELI is housed within the College of Arts and Sciences and, in addition to the director, is staffed by five full-time faculty administrators, three clerical support employees, and approximately 20 part-time instructors, of which roughly one third are considered adjuncts, another one third are doctoral students in the university's PhD program in second language acquisition and instructional technology, and the remaining one third consists of teaching assistants who are completing the 2-semester internship requirement for their MA program in applied linguistics. There is considerable instructor turnover due to the steady influx and attrition of students in the two aforementioned graduate programs. Thus, one of the main challenges faced by the program leadership is the continual need to orient new faculty to the

TABLE 1. DIFFERENCES BETWEEN A DISCRETE-SKILLS AND CISB CURRICULUM

Discrete Skills	*Content-Integrated / Skills-Based*
• Separate classes are devoted to the development of reading, writing, listening, and speaking skills	• Reading, writing, listening, and speaking skills are combined in every class
• The content of classes has lower priority than the skills which are targeted	• Course content is the vehicle through which language skills are integrated and taught
• Topics of study are often unrelated to each other	• Topics in every class are unified under one theme

rather unconventional pedagogical focus of the curriculum and help them adjust to it, but more importantly, to implement it effectively. To some extent, the same challenge presents itself with regard to orienting the IEP students to the CISB curriculum. The actual organization of the curriculum as well as ways in which the IEP has confronted the practical issues of implementation are addressed below.

◈ DESCRIPTION

What specifically was the catalyst that ignited the shift from a discrete skills curriculum to a CISB curriculum? Appropriately enough, it was the work of graduate students enrolled in a TESL curriculum design course at USF. Their charge was to follow all the steps prescribed by curriculum developers, except for program delivery:

1. conduct a needs analysis
2. formulate objectives
3. determine appropriate testing protocols
4. develop materials
5. deliver the program

The ELI was not only their venue but, for many, the only model they knew. Their project reflected the influence of earlier course work they had taken in second language acquisition research, methods, and testing.

These classes essentially built a case for a constructivist approach to second language learning and teaching, one that called for rich, natural input and plenty of opportunity for negotiation of meaning and the operation of a language acquisition device. The curriculum design students discovered that although many teachers at the ELI independently engaged in constructivist practices, the curriculum as a whole did not communicate a coherent constructivist philosophy. The irony was not lost on any of the parties, either in the curriculum design course or in the IEP, and steps were immediately taken to revisit the ELI curriculum and revise it appropriately. Mindful of the need to proceed thoughtfully and deliberately, however, the IEP's academic coordinator considered the many variables that must inform curricular reform, among them the concerns of administrators and teachers. The following emerged as the most salient issues:

- ELI graduates need university-admissible TOEFL scores.

- ELI students require preparation for Scholastic Aptitude Test, Graduate Record Exam, and Graduate Management Admission Test.

- ELI teachers and administrators were hesitant to make fundamental changes to the discrete skills curriculum for fear of: (a) failing to help students attain the minimum scores on the tests mentioned above, (b) weakening the academic rigor of the curriculum, (c) losing program accountability, and alienating students used to a more traditional format.

The heavy obligation of preparing students to function successfully in the academic programs of their choice tended to place constraints on the ELI's willingness to change. In particular, its leadership and faculty did not want learners to be adversely affected. They feared that the program would lose its pedagogical focus and become dangerously diffused if a variety of academic skills were to be woven together rather than treated separately. Although the group wanted to shift to a more holistic, authentic, and theoretically supportable curriculum, it faced significant pressure to consider the perceived disadvantages to its learners. The ELI's unique mission and make up also played an important role in planning for a change.

❖ DISTINGUISHING FEATURES

The ELI is similar to many other IEPs in that it is a self-supporting academic unit of the university. This affords it the freedom to experiment with new methods, and, in fact, demands it keep current with the latest research in second language acquisition and teaching. The ELI is special, though, in its service orientation and mission. It is primarily a place where novice teachers experiment with the tools of a new trade, experienced teachers hone their pedagogical skills, and scholars generate new knowledge about second language acquisition. Secondarily, but certainly not inconsequentially, it is a provider of effective ESL instruction to international students preparing to enter U.S. universities. The two functions go hand in hand.

As a clinical facility, the ELI is naturally integrated into the course work of the affiliated academic graduate programs through a host of laboratory projects, observation and practice teaching being the most common but also including such tasks as the creation and administration of testing materials and the assignment of ethnographic interviews. Similar to other research/teaching labs, professional development issues (e.g., mentoring, evaluation, innovation) are paramount.

Balancing the training and research aspects of the ELI's mission with instruction in English requires a special approach to language teaching and learning. Not only must the Institute meet the academic needs of the students, but it must also get students to buy into the approach. For most of the students, a curriculum that takes a CISB approach to language teaching is new and requires an adjustment on their part. Table 2 provides an overview of the curriculum.

Discrete Skills Overview

Grammar is one of the discrete skills taught at the ELI at all levels (see Table 3). Research has shown the benefits of explicit instruction in grammar (Long, 1983; Pavesi, 1986; Perkins & Larsen-Freeman, 1975; Pica, 1983, 1985; Pienemann, 1984; Schmidt, 1990). In addition, based on their experience with methods of instruction in their countries, students more often than not equate direct grammar instruction with language learning. Coupling research findings with students' expectations, then, resulted in including a separate grammar class in the curriculum.

Prior to the addition of a multimedia computer lab in autumn 1997, students received listening skills instruction in a traditional language laboratory. Once students were no longer sitting in carrels, classroom instruction became more communicative naturally. Listening-speaking instruction is now included in the first three levels in the curriculum. Students in Level IV receive authentic listening practice in their Cultural Contacts class via an outside classroom lecturer who speaks on topics related to U.S. culture: values, the educational system, religion, business, politics, and others.

TABLE 2. OVERVIEW OF THE ELI CURRICULUM

I	Basic Grammar	Cultural Contacts	Strategies for Learning	Literature	Listening/ Speaking
	Practice in producing basic grammatical forms in oral and written language	Reading, writing, and speaking about well-known places, people, foods, and holidays in the United States	Making use of communicative skills in a variety of contexts; building a basic vocabulary	Readings on a variety of themes; speaking and writing about experiences as they relate to those themes	Listening for the most common patterns of U.S. speech as they are found in basic communicative contexts Describing jobs, asking for/giving directions, and discussing health and illnesses

II Low Intermediate Grammar	Cultural Contacts	Strategies for Learning	Literature	Listening/ Speaking
Practice in the production of oral and written English grammar	Speaking and writing about U.S. customs and traditions as they compare to other cultures	Using resources in order to become more independent learners: library use, dictionary use, reading and writing strategies	Reading a variety of entertaining short stories; writing and speaking about the elements of literature as they are found in the stories	Listening to increasingly challenging conversations and lectures based on everyday themes Discussing related social and survival topics

III High Intermediate Grammar	Cultural Contacts	Electives	Electives	Listening/ Speaking
Practice in the production of more complex grammatical forms	Writing, speaking, and reading about popular films that depict contrasts between different cultures in the United States	1. Students from Levels III and IV are combined in courses that meet for 2 hours each day	2. Each elective course is 6 or 7 weeks long (half-semester) and meets each day	Listening to authentic pre-sentations on a variety of topics; taking notes Discussing contemporary political and social topics related to academic and non-academic settings.

IV Advanced Grammar	Cultural Contacts	Electives	Electives	Writing Lab
A survey of English grammar with emphasis on the pro-duction of more complex verb and sentence structures	Listening to university lectures on U.S. studies; reading and speaking about those topics	3. Students select their classes at the beginning of the term and at midterm	4. Elective classes have dealt with interests such as business, TOEFL, literature, pro-nunciation, idioms, current events, computer skills, and editing	Using computers to answer essay questions and do a research report on topics found in American Studies Cultural Contacts course

TABLE 3. ELI CURRICULUM SKILLS FOCUS OVERVIEW

Level	Discrete Skills	Content-based
I and II	Grammar Listening/Speaking	Literature Strategies for Learning Cultural Contacts
III	Grammar Listening/Speaking Electives	Cultural Contacts Electives
IV	Grammar Writing Electives	Cultural Contacts Electives

A separate writing skills class is included in Level IV. Students receive instruction in essay writing, improve their summarizing skills, and develop their research skills. The final components of the curriculum are the electives, some of which target discrete skills and some of which are content based.

Discrete and Content-Based Skills Overlap

The nature of the ELI curriculum allows students in the third and fourth levels to interact twice daily, one hour in the morning and one in the afternoon, throughout the semester via elective courses. Each elective is half a semester in length, allowing students to choose a total of four electives during the semester. Combining students from the two levels promotes interaction among students enrolled in the program and allows for a wider variety of courses to be offered. This variety includes electives that focus on discrete skills, namely, TOEFL Preparation, Writing Improvement Through Spelling, Reading for Pleasure, and Introduction to Public Speaking. Electives can also be content based: Writing for the Media (a student-produced newsletter), American English—Accents and Attitudes, Issues in the News, Computer Skills, and English Through Music are examples of the content-based courses offered regularly. Ideas for new elective offerings are suggested by the instructional staff or by the students themselves. Instructors are encouraged to submit proposals for courses and often create electives that allow them to share their expertise in a particular skill or subject area.

Content-Based Skills Overview

The remaining courses in the curriculum are content based. Cultural Contacts is offered at all four levels. Students in the first two levels focus primarily on the culture of the United States and share information about their cultures with their classmates orally and in writing. Students in the two upper levels explore the culture of the United States more deeply and, through discussion and writing, share features of their cultures with classmates.

In addition to the Cultural Contacts classes, students in the first two levels are also enrolled in a content-based series of classes called Literature and Strategies for Learning. In Literature, students read short stories, focusing on grammar, vocabulary, and reading skills, and the elements of literature.

The Strategies for Learning classes reflect the belief that students can become more effective in their language learning when exposed to explicit strategy instruction and when the strategies themselves are integrated into the lessons (Flaitz, Feyten, Fox, & Mukherjee, 1995). Students in the first level work on developing vocabulary skills; students in the second level are exposed to resources that will help them become more independent learners: an English-English dictionary and the library as a source of information for a short research project. At the same time, they learn and practice reading strategies and begin acquiring academic writing skills.

Integration of Skills

As much as possible throughout the curriculum, there is an integration of listening, speaking, reading, and writing skills in each class. Across a level, the focus on a particular skill in each class may change, but all of the skills are addressed. Instructors plan for this integration of skills using a list of specific course objectives. In addition, skill integration is enhanced by selecting integrated skills textbooks that fit the goals and objectives outlined in the curriculum.

The variation in skill emphasis is most clearly evident in Cultural Contacts classes. In the first level, students focus largely on reading but begin developing their writing and speaking skills as well. As students progress to the second level, the focus changes to improving speaking skills. Students make oral presentations at the end of the semester based on written reports developed in their Strategies for Learning class. Cultural Contacts at the third level emphasizes writing skills; students write about cultural contrasts found in films and develop their listening and speaking skills in this class as well. Finally, in the fourth level, the focus of the class returns to reading, but students also listen to lectures, practice note-taking skills, and share in group discussions.

Academic preparation of the student is the goal that shapes instruction at all levels. With the addition of the multimedia lab in fall 1997, integration of skills took on a completely new meaning and required reviewing the curriculum to determine the best use of the computer lab. The ELI computer lab curriculum reflects the effort to consider all aspects of the students' program of study and to identify ways in which the resources of the lab may be exploited for second language acquisition purposes. The lab component reinforces skills and knowledge acquired in other areas of the curriculum and enhances learning opportunities by extending the range and variety of learning tasks and resources. In addition, it enables students to make use of authentic materials designed for use by native-English-speaking computer users. Finally, it increases students' comfort with computer technology. Integration of the computer lab into classes is depicted in Table 4.

Seminar in Academic Skills

In January 1998, the ELI began offering a bridge course titled Seminar in Academic Skills. Composed of modules, the course focuses on developing academic reading and writing skills beyond the general skills addressed in Levels I–IV. Students enrolled in the seminar write a research paper on a topic related to their major field of study. Readings focus on authentic college material, with selections from various disciplines, and writing practice ranges from developing essays for college applications to answering essay test questions to analyzing ideas presented in a reading. The

TABLE 4. ELI COMPUTER LAB / CURRICULUM INTEGRATION

	Level	Classes		Total Hours/Week
I and II	Listening/Speaking— 1 hour per week	Strategies for Learning— 1 hour for Strategies; 1 hour for General Lab		3
III	Listening/Speaking— 1 hour per week	Cultural Contacts— 2 hours per week	Afternoon elective—1 hour per week for General Lab	4
IV	Writing Lab— 2 hours per week	Afternoon elective— 1 hour per week for General Lab		3

modules Introduction to the University and Lectures are combined, and, through informal agreements with university faculty, students are able to attend a university class throughout the semester. Sitting in on a class not only presents students with and involves them in the culture of the U.S. classroom, but also gives them practical experience in reading large amounts of material, taking notes during a lecture, and preparing for and taking a variety of tests. Students continue to practice developing their oral skills while enrolled in the seminar through group projects, oral presentations, and classroom discussions. Grammar instruction is integrated into all of the modules of the seminar.

◈ PRACTICAL IDEAS

Integrating the various components of the curriculum to best meet student needs and program goals required a period of trial and error, and regular curriculum evaluations and adjustments continue to be made. There was no precedent for a CISB curriculum, and, with no model to follow, program administrators and instructors relied on research and input from each other to guide them in the creation of the curriculum. What follows are some practical suggestions for implementing a CISB curriculum such as ours.

Orient Students to the CISB Curriculum

Students first learn about the ELI's CISB curriculum during student orientation on their second day on campus. Each student receives a copy of the ELI student handbook, which begins with a section on language learning and contains information about specific ELI program requirements and policies.

Students are introduced to the CISB curriculum through the use of metaphor. Each student receives a drawing of an empty house (see Appendix A), and as students learn about the curriculum, they explore their new surroundings and furnish their house with information about the classes. For example, the sidewalk to the house represents Grammar, and the garden Cultural Contacts. Each floor of the house represents a level at the ELI, and each is furnished somewhat differently.

Each part of the curriculum is briefly explained, with particular emphasis on the fact that the four skills of listening, speaking, reading, and writing will be practiced in all of their classes, thus making their classes integrated. They also learn that some skills receive more focus in one class than another. Literature, for example, will focus largely on reading skills. By the time the house is complete, students are more comfortable with the idea that their classes may be different from those they are used to, and when students receive their class schedules at the end of orientation, there are no surprises. Students take home the completed house and can refer to it as they go over their class schedule. By the time they begin classes the next day, they are already familiar with a class titled Strategies for Learning or Cultural Contacts.

Instructors follow up the general orientation to the curriculum with more in-depth explanations and information during the first day and week of classes.

Organize Electives to Offer the Widest Variety Possible

The number of electives offered is determined by the number of sections (15 students per section) for Levels III and IV. Combining the two levels for electives allows students an opportunity to meet and mix with students from other sections and other levels, and it offers a wider variety of electives to choose from as well. Although there are skill and ability differences between Level III and IV students, instructors and students both rise to meet the challenge those differences present in order to retain the benefit of a wider selection of electives.

A few days before elective registration, students receive a registration form and a description sheet containing a short explanation of each elective and textbook requirements. The registration form lists all the morning and afternoon electives and asks students to make first, second, and sometimes, third choices. A note at the bottom of the form explains that students who do not get their first elective choice may request that their names be put on a waiting list and that if numbers warrant it, an additional section of that elective will be offered.

Ensure That Texts are Suitable for a CISB Curriculum

We are careful to include various kinds of textbooks: texts written specifically for ESL, texts that are low vocabulary-high interest and written for adult native English speakers, texts that are content based, and texts that focus on discrete skills. Textbooks are chosen based on course objectives and teacher input, but students also have an opportunity to comment on texts through a course evaluation filled out at the end of each semester. Preferred texts most often include those integrating skills and those with content-based formats. Alternating two sets of texts from one semester to the next ensures that students who repeat a level are not bored with material already covered and gives teachers a chance to integrate new activities and ideas.

Integrate Computer Skills Into the Curriculum Rather Than Add Them

The goal in integrating computer skills into the curriculum was to link classes in the computer lab to existing classes resulting in enhancement of the class and opportunities for students to improve a skill deemed weak by a student's instructors. As noted in Table 4, all listening-speaking classes meet in the lab 1 hour a week. Students typically use a software program for listening practice, but Internet activities using real audio are commonly assigned. Strategies classes work on typing skills, word-processing skills, and library research skills. Students in the third-level Cultural Contacts class and fourth-level Writing Lab class work on composition and word-processing skills.

Students receive additional skills practice during General Lab; assignments can be prescribed by the instructor for that class, by any of the students' other four instructors or by the students themselves. Afternoon electives usually focus on using software to work on vocabulary, reading, or listening skills. Students also prepare for the TOEFL exam by using TOEFL preparation software or by practicing timed writing. In addition to the above schedule, a morning computer skills elective is offered to students in the third and fourth levels. Students learn and practice Microsoft Word, e-mail, Internet, and PowerPoint skills in this class.

Integrate Authentic Language Practice Into the Curriculum

Students ask for and expect interaction with native speakers of English during their term of study in the United States. In addition to extracurricular opportunities, including a conversation partners program and trips to area attractions, students are exposed to real language in authentic contexts. We offer a guest lecture series that has featured the mayor of the city of Tampa, among other speakers. In addition, we often invite campus and community personnel to speak with students and have round-table discussions in class. Recently, all Cultural Contacts classes participated in a workshop on dating in the United States, presented by an advisor from International Student and Scholar Services. Listening/Speaking III students have been given the opportunity to observe a Mass Communications class at USF, and the Seminar class has audited a developmental psychology course all semester.

Link Field Trips to Instructional Content

The success of educationally oriented field trips can be greatly increased with in-class preparation the week prior to the outing. Typically, Listening/Speaking or Cultural Contacts teachers are assigned to prepare students. The Assistant Director for Curriculum provides instructors with background information on the destination (e.g., Florida Aquarium, Dalí Museum, or Kennedy Space Center), develops sample activities from which to choose, and offers suggestions for creating others. Students use the background information in activities before and during the trip. In one instance, students were given a list of items to look for while touring Tampa's Henry B. Plant Museum. During the trip, they wrote down the name of the room in which they found the object and brought the assignment to class the next day for a follow-up activity.

Use Faculty Meetings and In-Service Workshops to Reinforce CISB Curricular Objectives

Teachers are given ample opportunity to add to their knowledge base, refine their teaching skills, and participate actively in bringing about curricular change through a variety of forums. For example, the first faculty meeting of the semester may address a particular skill, focusing on its integration into each of the classes, or, alternatively, it may address one particular class, focusing on ways to effectively integrate the four skills into that class. Early in the semester, new instructors attend in-service workshops to familiarize them with the computer lab, its programs, and types of activities that foster integration of skills. These workshops are presented by the institute director, administrators, or faculty and sometimes by faculty from the affiliated academic unit. Likewise, teachers can participate in professional development workshops given by visiting leaders in the field of ESL.

Plan Level Meetings to Promote Collaboration and Sharing

Throughout the semester, regularly scheduled level meetings allow instructors to share information about students, activities, and curriculum matters. Meetings are scheduled by level. For example, all of the Level I instructors or all of the Level IV instructors meet to discuss the students in their sections.

Many instructors continue to meet informally until midterm when they gather to discuss students' progress and their midterm reports. Instructors meet again at the end of the semester to go over end-of-term procedures and offer general comments on and recommendations for the program. A typical semester includes seven meetings. Attendance is required of all instructors, and meetings usually last 30 minutes.

Acknowledge the Investment of Time and Effort
Needed to Implement the Curriculum

The vast majority of instructors at the ELI work as part-time adjunct faculty, meaning that they receive no medical or retirement benefits, and there is scant job security. Therefore, a combination of intrinsic and extrinsic rewards must be carefully considered. After estimating the average number of hours that our instructors spend outside of class working on institute business, we built into each instructor's pay an extra stipend for service. We also attempt to provide support for conference attendance and other efforts to develop professionally. Birthdays are typically celebrated with a cake baked by one of the head administrators, and golf shirts bearing the ELI logo are presented to incoming faculty as a gesture of welcome. Last but not least, those who are on the front line in terms of implementation of this innovative and challenging curriculum are treated with respect, and the value of their contribution is clearly and frequently articulated.

❖ CONCLUSION

Four years after the implementation of the new CISB curriculum, an effort was made to assess its effectiveness with the following research question: Is there a difference in achievement on the CELT (Comprehensive English Language Test) between the students studying under the discrete skills curriculum and those studying under the CISB curriculum? Working with an Incentive Grant from University and College Intensive English Programs (UCIEP), the ELI sought to compare pre- and posttest scores on CELT over a 3-year period immediately preceding the curriculum shift (1990, 1991, 1992) with those over a 3-year period after the change (1994, 1995, 1996).

A repeated measures ANOVA analyzed four factors:

1. approach: discrete skills or CISB
2. level: beginning, low intermediate, high intermediate, or advanced
3. time: pretest or posttest
4. test component: listening, grammar, and vocabulary

The clearest result that emerged from the data analysis was that students studying under both curricula improved over time. This is neither surprising nor enlightening.

When the approach factor by time interaction was examined, no significance was discovered. In other words, the difference between pre- and posttest scores was not affected by the curricular approach. The CISB group made no greater progress than did the discrete-skills group. Additional interactions were examined—level × time, approach × level × time, level × test component, approach × level × test component—but none of these analyses produced differences that were statistically significant. In a word, the change from a discrete skills curriculum to a CISB curriculum did not adversely affect the ELI students' performance on the CELT.

The degree to which fluency, productivity, authenticity, motivation, and other essential language skills increased has been left to anecdotal accounts. For example, students are believed to memorize less and use language more. After the change, there were fewer student requests for level changes, perhaps due to the greater possibility for a CISB curriculum to accommodate a wider variety of student abilities and preferences. The classes now lend themselves more readily to the use of authentic materials and to special projects that involve students more in the life of the campus and broader community. In the upper levels, both students and teachers have more input into what will be taught as well. These perceived benefits, in combination with the empirical data, show that a CISB curriculum provides a strong philosophical base upon which to help students prepare for life after the ELI.

◈ CONTRIBUTORS

Barbara Smith-Palinkas is assistant director for Curriculum and Instruction of the English Language Institute at the University of South Florida, in the United States. She received her master's degree in English with a specialization in applied English linguistics from the University of Wisconsin–Madison.

Donna M. Tortorella is an adjunct instructor of ESL at the English Language Institute and a mentor for graduate interns in the MA applied linguistics program at the University of South Florida. She received her undergraduate degree at Framingham State College, Framingham, Massachusetts, and her MA TESOL at Fairleigh Dickinson University, Madison, New Jersey.

Jeffra Flaitz is director of the English Language Institute at the University of South Florida (USF). She is also a member of the graduate faculty in USF's programs in applied linguistics (MA) and second language acquisition and instructional technology (PhD). She received her doctorate and master's degree in TESOL from the State University of New York at Buffalo.

❖ APPENDIX A

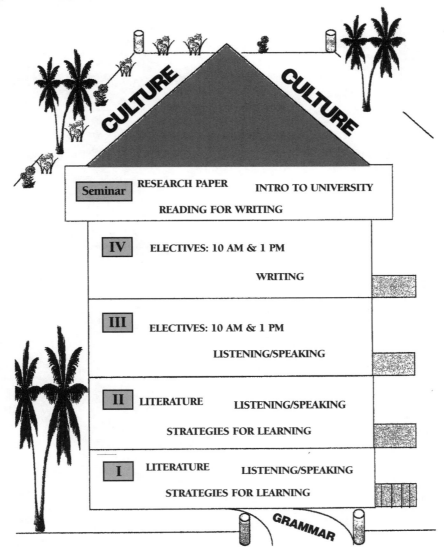

CHAPTER 3

Initiating Students Into the Academic Community

Maria Dantas-Whitney, Ann Lindsay Larson,
and Barbara Tolley Dowling

❖ INTRODUCTION

The English Language Institute (ELI) at Oregon State University, in the United States, faces constant challenges. On the administrative side, because of its self-supporting nature, it struggles with issues related to financial planning, marketing, and recruitment. In addition, as a nontraditional (i.e., non-degree-granting) unit on campus, it must represent the interests of its students and faculty within the larger university community.

On the instructional side, the ELI faces different types of challenges. Because its mission is to prepare international students for undergraduate and graduate degree programs at U.S. colleges or universities, merely teaching students the forms and functions of the English language is not enough. The ELI's job is also to help students become socialized into, or "apprenticed into" (Gee, 1990, p. 147) the academic discourse. Zamel (1991) reminds us that the academic discourse community represents a separate cultural community "with its own set of expectations, assumptions and conventions" (p. 10). Our mission is to help our students acquire the skills and knowledge that will enable them to succeed in this new culture. To this end, the ELI curriculum has traditionally focused on a variety of skills and competencies:

- language skills: Our curriculum combines reading, writing, listening, and speaking in an integrated skills approach. In the lower proficiency levels, our approach is task based and thematic. As students become more advanced, they move into a more content-based curriculum. In addition, we offer stand-alone modules that focus on specific language areas such as grammar, TOEFL preparation, and pronunciation. The ELI curriculum, therefore, could be described as a hybrid (Stoller, 1999).

- study skills and strategies: Along with language skills, the ELI emphasizes study skills, such as planning an outline for a composition, summarizing an article, or predicting the content of a video. In addition, we incorporate activities that promote student independence and self-direction (Dantas-Whitney & Larson, 2000; Nunan, 1998).

- cognitive skills: Cognitive flexibility, critical and analytical thinking, problem-solving and other "higher order thinking skills" (Johns, 1992, p. 67) are also developed through many of our class activities.

- affective factors: When designing classroom tasks and assignments, we take into consideration affective factors such as increasing student motivation and self-esteem. These factors play a very important role in fostering student social adjustment and general well-being, which are essential elements for academic achievement (Westwood, 1990).

In the fall of 1993 we decided to critically review the ELI curriculum. We realized that the skills mentioned above were essential components of our courses, but we asked ourselves if what we were doing was enough to prepare students for the complex demands of the university community.

As we examined our six-level curriculum, we noticed that many of our courses incorporated activities that served as bridges into the university, such as listening to lectures and doing library research. However, these activities were often short-term and reserved for the most proficient students. Many times, because they were not spiraled throughout the curriculum (i.e., there were gaps and some duplication), they did not adequately prepare students for a smooth transition into the academic community.

We then formed a task force and made a conscious and systematic effort to create academic bridges at every level of our curriculum. We would still emphasize all the skills previously taught in our curriculum, but we would incorporate authentic links with the university whenever possible, following a careful sequence so the activities would build upon each other as students advanced through our levels. In this chapter, we summarize a series of tasks and activities that were developed for this purpose. We illustrate how these activities are woven throughout the curriculum in order to initiate students gradually into the university system.

We describe several academic preparation activities and courses that have been implemented in all levels of the ELI. These include tasks that enable students to become acquainted with and exploit university resources (Johns, 1992), such as the health center and campus study areas, and activities that encourage students to interact with different members of the university community as they participate in field visits, gather and synthesize information, and do observations. These activities follow a gradual progression. As students become more proficient, they attend a sheltered course with English language support and observe university classes in their chosen fields of study.

◈ CONTEXT

The ELI is part of Oregon State University (OSU), a large land, sea, and space grant research university of approximately 17,000 students located in Corvallis, Oregon. Within OSU, the ELI is an autonomous unit under the Office of International Programs. The ELI director and teachers are OSU faculty with non-tenure-track contracts (i.e., instructor and senior instructor ranks). Of the approximately 130 students enrolled at the ELI each quarter, about one third are graduate students, and two thirds are undergraduates. Approximately 30% of ELI students are conditionally admitted to OSU and, therefore, study part-time at the ELI and part-time at OSU. All ELI students have full access to OSU facilities, such as the library, computer centers, recreation centers, and student events.

◈ DESCRIPTION

The ELI curriculum task force attempted to answer this question: How should student initiation into the academic community be incorporated throughout the curriculum? As an English for academic purposes (EAP) program, the ELI, of course, offered several classes and activities to prepare students for success in a U.S. university setting. However, the academic preparation activities and linkages tended to be clustered in the two highest levels of the six-level program. In addition, these activities had not been examined holistically across our curriculum to ensure appropriate sequencing and spiraling of skills. The primary mandate for this task force was, therefore, to evaluate and recommend more direct linkages at all proficiency levels to university courses and the campus community.

The task force, made up of our academic coordinator and five instructors, worked on its mandate for approximately 7 months. We involved the entire staff as much as possible in developing recommendations. The first step was to survey ELI teachers to find out what specific activities in their course syllabi had provided our students with direct linkages to the university. In addition to clearly documenting the status quo and finding out which activities had been successfully implemented, we wanted to see if any gaps or overlaps existed. We also knew that some activities had been tied to individual instructors and their university contacts, and when staffing changes were made, some of these academic bridges were not maintained. One of the goals of the Curriculum Task Force was to institutionalize these linkages so that they would continue as a part of the curriculum regardless of staffing.

As the task force evolved, our objectives became more clearly defined. We determined that

- academic linkages needed to be institutionalized and carefully sequenced throughout the ELI's six-level curriculum

- the curricular changes at the lower levels would add to or modify existing course descriptions, but at the higher levels some new courses would be proposed and developed

- these campus linkages needed to be offered outside the classroom as well because cocurricular linkages are critical to students' initial transition to and their ultimate success in the university

The resulting recommendations were as follows:

1. Linkages to campus facilities/activities and academic preparation should begin at Level 1 and be spiraled throughout the various levels in order to gradually initiate ELI students into U.S. university culture.

2. The integrated courses at the lowest three levels should incorporate more campus activities and experiences.

3. Level 4 courses should include a sheltered content unit taught by an expert in an academic field in conjunction with ELI instructors.

4. Courses at Levels 5 and 6 should build on the campus linkages developed in the lower levels and place increasing emphasis on academic preparation activities. Two new courses, a guided observation and an adjunct course, would be added to the curriculum.

5.   All activities should be coordinated to avoid duplication and to ensure spiraling of content and skills.

6.   A cocurricular task force should be formed to review all nonclassroom components of our program (e.g., orientation sessions, e-mail workshops, advising seminars and activities with conversation partners) and increase ELI student participation in OSU recreational activities, student organizations and clubs, residence hall events, and other programs, such as the writing center and workshops conducted by the student health center.

After both task forces completed their work, we compiled a detailed list of campus linkages and academic preparation activities being offered to ELI students in and out of the classroom. Figure 1 provides a graphic representation of how academic preparation and campus interactions are now woven throughout the ELI program. As illustrated, students bring to our program their own background knowledge from previous academic, social, and cultural experiences, which represent foundations upon which their future academic development is built (Cummins, 1996). At the ELI, they participate in a variety of activities in beginning- through advanced-level courses designed to ease their transition into the university community. We hope that these students will use their newly acquired skills and knowledge to succeed in their academic endeavors when they leave the ELI and matriculate into a college or university.

◈ DISTINGUISHING FEATURES
Beginning Levels 1 and 2

At the beginning levels, our strategy is to adapt existing units to include more academic content and tasks. The emphasis is on getting the students out of the classroom, orienting them to campus facilities and activities, and helping them acquire the basic language skills needed to participate in the activities. These tasks include visits to the student health and recreation centers, exploration of eating establishments on and around campus, comparisons of different housing options, and interviews with university students about campus life.

The materials we developed are highly structured and task based. An example of a common unit found in most basic language materials is describing a room. Instead of having students describe their bedrooms or the classroom, we now take groups of students on visits to different study areas on campus. They draw a diagram of a study area and write a description of it. As a follow-up activity, students can discuss the advantages and disadvantages of each of the study areas, compare their diagrams and descriptions, and decide where they would like to study. In preparation for this task-based activity, students practice names of furniture and parts of a room, prepositions of location, and other grammatical structures that will be needed to describe a study area. They also read short articles about what makes a good study atmosphere, watch videos describing various locations, and interview U.S. students regarding their study habits. This unit can also be expanded to include exercises in reading a campus map and locating the study areas.

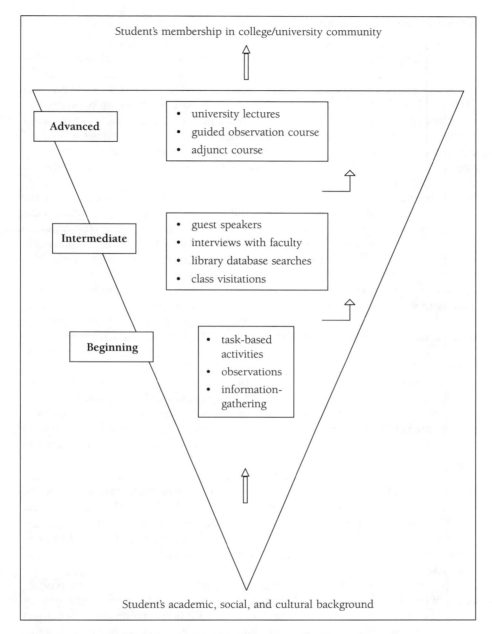

Student's membership in college/university community

Advanced
- university lectures
- guided observation course
- adjunct course

Intermediate
- guest speakers
- interviews with faculty
- library database searches
- class visitations

Beginning
- task-based activities
- observations
- information-gathering

Student's academic, social, and cultural background

FIGURE 1. Examples of University-Link Activities Spiraling Throughout the ELI Curriculum

Intermediate Levels 3 and 4

Low intermediate-level students explore the university community in a variety of ways. Students complete assignments that include a tour of the campus radio/TV station, conduct guided research in the library, listen to guest speakers from the student health center or other departments, and interview OSU students on a variety of topics. Toward the end of the quarter, students choose an OSU class to observe for one class session. After receiving the professor's permission, they sit in on one class meeting and observe teacher and student behavior in order to answer a series of structured and focused questions about student conduct in a U.S. university classroom. Later, in their ELI class, students discuss their observations and make cultural comparisons.

High intermediate-level students develop further links with members of the OSU community through a discovery project in their listening-speaking class (Dantas-Whitney, 1998). Through this term-long project, they thoroughly explore a topic of their choice and, in the process, learn a great deal about U.S. culture and values. During the first part of this project, they interview 10 people, often U.S. university students, and then summarize and interpret their findings for their classmates in a poster session. The culminating activity is to interview an expert, often a professor or a campus administrator. Through this project, students have made direct contact with future professors and other members of the university community well before they actually become full-time university students.

Mini-Sheltered Course

High intermediate-level students also participate in a short, simulated university lecture class. This mini-sheltered course (Dantas-Whitney & Larson, 1996) is similar in many ways to an actual university course: Students take lecture notes, read articles, take short essay exams, and write a research paper. Through ESL support classes, they gain the language and study skills necessary to succeed in the content class.

Our mini-sheltered course comprises three lectures given by a university professor. Over the years, we have chosen to explore two themes: Native Americans, with lectures presented by anthropology professors; and Personal Skills for Academic Success, with lectures given by psychologists from the university counseling office. These lectures are well organized, clearly presented and typical of introductory-level university lectures. Much as they would in an actual university class, students listen, take notes, and ask and answer questions.

The 4.5 hours of university lectures provide the content focus for more than 25 hours of language development. Prelecture activities in the ESL support class provide students with the conceptual framework necessary for understanding lecture content and strengthen vocabulary and listening and note-taking skills. In debriefing sessions, students discuss the content of the lecture, study difficult vocabulary items, and develop study and test taking skills as they prepare for an exam on language and ideas from the lectures. Follow-up activities include watching videos, interviewing experts, and engaging in library research on themes introduced in the lectures. Through these activities students gain the broad understanding and the detailed in-depth knowledge they need to complete the culminating activities for this class: research papers, simulations, and formal oral presentations.

This mini-sheltered model has been easy to implement because it fits within our existing EAP curriculum. Both the ESL support and the lectures take place within the students' regular listening-speaking and reading-writing courses, providing a focus for content integration among the intermediate-level classes. Most important, this short lecture course encourages students to take a critical step toward university adjustment at a relatively early stage in their language development. In a warm, nonthreatening atmosphere, students gain a realistic view of the demands they will face as university students.

Advanced Levels 5 and 6

Much more than in lower levels, our advanced students had always listened to guest speakers, attended lectures and other university functions, interviewed students and faculty members, and used university resources and facilities in order to fulfill course assignments. Even though university linkages had been an integral part of our advanced levels, the Curriculum Task Force felt that our advanced students needed more prolonged and direct university experiences and decided to add new bridge courses to our curriculum. We first added a guided observation and an adjunct course, and we later created an advanced sheltered course. Although these courses differed in design, focus, and content, they shared the objective of providing extended authentic university classroom experiences.

Guided Observation

This academic orientation course centers around firsthand observation and analysis of an actual university class. Under the direction of an ELI instructor, students select and sit in on a term-long, lower division undergraduate class in a subject area of their choice. They are not required to buy textbooks, write papers, or take exams. Their primary role is to take lecture notes and observe classroom interactions.

In a concurrent 3-hour per week EAP support class, the students prepare for and interpret their university classroom experiences. Topics of this academic orientation course include introduction to university procedures, development of cross-cultural awareness in an academic setting, strategies for minimizing academic adjustment problems, and refinement of study skills. Students strengthen language and study skills through note-taking practice, discussion, oral presentations, reading, writing, and watching videos. Using response journals or electronic discussion boards, they analyze professor and student interactions in their OSU classes, classroom atmosphere, and different course assignments. On a very practical level, they read a university bulletin, plan a sample course of study from the schedule of classes, and fill out an actual application form. They examine course syllabi, analyze midterm and final examinations from a variety of disciplines, and interview fellow OSU students on study habits and class expectations. The class is enriched by guest speakers, such as a foreign student advisor who discusses academic adjustment issues and panels of international and U.S. students who describe their own university experiences.

This course offers several advantages to ELI students. As an elective, Guided Observation does not replace a core language class. Instead, the observation experience serves as a powerful motivator for language learning in their other ELI classes as students gain a realistic view of the demands they will face in dealing with difficult content material in a second language. Because study is not tied to a specific content, students can select a university course according to their individual interests and begin to learn in advance the content and specialized language of their major. Because no university credit is attached, they are able to ease their way into the academic community without the pressure of competing for grades.

Because Guided Observation makes use of existing university classes and resources, it does not require a large investment in time and money. An agreement worked out with the Office of Academic Affairs allows ELI students to observe OSU classes without registering or paying auditing fees.

Adjunct Course

Another recommendation of the Curriculum Task Force was that an adjunct course be added to our curriculum, not as an elective but as a core class that students could select in place of another advanced-level requirement. This course was designed for academically admissible students whose TOEFL scores ranged from slightly below 500–550. Our adjunct model was similar to that of many other IEP programs: Students took an undergraduate course with OSU students for academic credit while simultaneously taking a 3-hour/week English language support class.

We selected an introductory sociology class as our university course because it met several important criteria. First, its content was helpful to students trying to adapt to a new culture. It was a general education course that could be applied toward an undergraduate degree and was primarily a lecture class that would require high-level note-taking skills. Also, it had a high enough enrollment that our ESL students would not represent a disproportionate part of the class. The class was taught by a professor who was enthusiastic about working with our students but would not compromise his high standards because of their participation. The textbook was well organized, clear, and fairly easy to comprehend.

The main purpose of the parallel ELI support class was to develop language and study skills to facilitate learning in the OSU class. The support class had an integrated skills approach with emphasis on note-taking, reading, and writing. Class materials included the text from the OSU class, supplementary materials provided by the professor, and specially designed ESL materials. Some class time was devoted to cultural explanations about the language used in the classroom, teacher expectations, and effective classroom behavior. Most of class time, however, was spent on the content of the OSU course. Although they were not directly focusing on language most of the time, the students effectively acquired the language and study skills they needed in order to pass difficult midterm and final exams. To this end, they worked as a team forming study groups, sharing class notes and coaching each other before tests. Almost all were successful, receiving final grades of A or B.

From a pedagogical point of view, this paired OSU/adjunct course was extremely successful. Of all of our university linkages, this experience was the most authentic. Our students were fully participating members of an actual university class, working for academic credit along side other university students. However, course enrollment was always low, primarily because of additional application and tuition fees and, therefore, the ELI administration could no longer justify offering it after the second year.

Advanced Sheltered Course

The adjunct module was replaced by a 6-hour-per-week sheltered course, taught to ELI students only. This course followed the model of our mini-sheltered course, but was much more intensive and lasted for an entire quarter. Building upon the relationship previously established through the adjunct course, we invited the same sociology professor to teach an abridged version of his sociology course to our ELI students once a week. Remaining class time was spent preparing for and debriefing after the lectures and developing academic language and study skills. As in our other bridge courses, special attention was given to analyzing cultural expectations and behavior in the classroom. One of the weaknesses of this model was that ELI students did not regularly interact with other OSU students. To compensate for this problem partially, we set up a project that paired OSU sociology students with ELI sheltered students in completing a course assignment. Even so, we recognized that this course did not provide students with the same depth of experience as the full immersion approach of the adjunct course.

However, the sheltered model did have some clear advantages. It served the needs of most advanced ELI students, both graduate and undergraduate, regardless of their intentions to pursue an academic degree at OSU. Because this course did not bear OSU credit, there were no additional registration requirements or fees for students. This new sheltered course also built needed flexibility into our advanced curriculum: It provided an additional bridge for Level 5 and 6 students who were academically bound. The class was, therefore, always fully enrolled.

◈ PRACTICAL IDEAS

It has now been 7 years since the ELI Curriculum Task Force first examined the question of how best to initiate students into the academic discourse community. During this time, we have regularly evaluated the innovations implemented by the task force, based on student and teacher feedback, administrative needs, and general changes to the institutional environment (e.g., changing demographics and enrollment trends). We would like to suggest practical ideas for programs embarking on similar endeavors. We discuss general considerations, implementation guidelines, and potential constraints for other IEPs to consider in their own contexts and situations.

General Considerations

Start at the Beginning Levels

Even with very limited language skills, students can engage in task-based activities that help them explore the academic environment. Language learning becomes more relevant because these activities are directly tied to their future academic goals.

Design Carefully Sequenced Activities

Tasks should gradually build upon one another, with campus interactions becoming more complex as the students' skills develop. At the ELI, for example, we found that participation in the mini-sheltered course in the high intermediate level was extremely helpful in preparing students for the advanced adjunct course.

Keep Current With the Requirements of University Courses and Adjust the IEP Curriculum to Fit Changing Demands

As Ferris (1998) points out, it is essential to examine the "academic contexts to which ESL students will be going in order to prepare them most effectively for the tasks that await them" (p. 311). For example, in our case, a universitywide writing across the curriculum program created a need for us to put more emphasis on timed writing assignments in the IEP classes.

Help Students Build Learning Strategies

It is important to keep in mind that IEP courses "cannot prepare students for *all* the academic contingencies that they may face" (Johns, 1992, p. 65, emphasis added). Because university classroom contexts and requirements vary greatly from discipline to discipline, it is impossible to predict the full range of academic tasks our students will encounter. Therefore, it is crucial for students to develop strategies that will enable them to plan, monitor and evaluate their learning (Chamot, Barnhardt, El-Dinary, & Robbins, 1999) in a variety of tasks and contexts.

Include Curricular and Cocurricular Links

Both curricular and cocurricular aspects of the program should be considered when developing links to the university. Adaptation to the campus community depends on social ties and other affective factors as much as academic preparation and linguistic skills.

Consider the Timing of Proposed Changes

The timing of these curricular and cocurricular changes is extremely important because most IEPs are part of a larger educational environment. For example, we took advantage of a major undergraduate curriculum revision at OSU as an external mandate for the implementation of more academic bridges. On the other hand, a period of declining enrollment and revenues such as occurred in the late 1990s in many IEPs might not be an opportune time to begin a major change effort (Dowling & McDougal, 1990; Stoller, 1997; Stoynoff, 1989).

Dare to Dream

Successful change efforts require strong advocates who dare to dream. In discussing the feasibility of creating guided observation and adjunct courses, we eventually decided to recommend incorporating both types of courses in the revised curricular blueprint. Even though the OSU administration had not been receptive to some of our curricular proposals in the past, this time both courses were supported and approved.

Implementation Guidelines

Involve staff at all levels of the IEP

A lot of energy and enthusiasm is needed to make major program changes. If administrators, teachers, and support staff participate in all stages of the change process, they take increased ownership of the innovations and are more motivated to carry them out.

Delineate all University Linkages and Academic Preparation Activities Clearly

As we implemented changes at the ELI, we produced a flow chart that displayed academic linkages being emphasized at each level. This chart was extremely effective in helping teachers coordinate class assignments to ensure curricular coherence within and across levels.

Conduct Regular Review and Evaluation of Curricular Innovations

It is important to set up curricular task forces to check if university links are working, if they are being woven throughout, and if they need to be modified (e.g., if a course has low enrollment, it might need to be revised in order to attract more students).

Contact Members of Different Campus Units

Faculty members from different departments can serve as coteachers of a sheltered or adjunct course. Staff members of different units can also be guest speakers or help set up activities. For example, OSU career counselors help us organize class visits to the university career placement office, and OSU librarians conduct research workshops for our students every term. University administrators are also great resources for the IEP (e.g., the OSU Director of Undergraduate Academic Programs approved our Guided Observation course, and the chair of the English department helped us obtain credit status for two advanced writing classes). These contacts not only enrich the curriculum but also increase the IEP's visibility on campus (Smith-Murdock, 1997).

Encourage Former IEP Students to Continue to Participate in the Life of the Institute

At the ELI, we ask some of our former students to attend classes and serve as expert informants about university demands, and we enlist their help in greeting and orienting new students. In our experience, former students have served as wonderful role models for current students who are struggling in their adaptation to the academic culture.

Involve University Students in IEP Activities

At our program, OSU students are employed as lab and office assistants. In addition, many of them participate in our conversation partner program. When these university students interact with our IEP students, new friendships and social bonds are established and become important support systems.

Encourage IEP Students to Participate in University Events

The ELI organizes student groups to attend different university functions such as dorm-sponsored parties and intramural sports. Participation in these functions is important in helping create a sense of belonging for IEP students within the larger university community.

Potential Constraints

As with any other change process, we must be aware of potential constraints that could work against successful implementation of ideas. In our case, lower enrollments and tight budgets brought about by the Asian economic crisis of the late 1990s forced the ELI to drop or modify some academic bridges. We now no longer offer the adjunct course, and we have temporarily stopped offering the advanced sheltered course in order to increase flexibility in student placement. However, despite setbacks, bridge activities are still an integral part of our curriculum. We have found that certain types of linkage activities have continued to be extremely successful: those which fit comfortably into our existing curriculum (e.g., mini-sheltered course), allow for flexibility and student choice (e.g., Guided Observation course) and are financially feasible for the institute. Now, with enrollment stabilizing, we look forward to reestablishing some of our bridge activities and creating new ones.

◈ CONCLUSION

Our new campus linkages have greatly enriched the ELI. We have witnessed firsthand the challenges international students encounter in university classes and, as a result, have become more focused and effective in our teaching. We have formed new relationships within the academic community by negotiating for and implementing new bridge courses. As a result of these new ties, the ELI's goals and needs have become more widely understood, and the ELI has become a more integral part of the campus.

The university has also benefited. Like other large state universities, OSU faces a challenge in retaining students: Approximately 16% of first-year students do not return the following year. Generally, international students face all the difficulties that U.S. students do, with the additional problems of adjusting to a new culture and functioning in a foreign university environment. Unlike newly arrived international OSU students, however, matriculating ELI students feel at home on campus and in the university classroom and, as a result, are less likely to face overwhelming adjustment problems. We believe that the university community has been enriched through the new connections created by our academic linkage activities. Professors who have taught our sheltered and adjunct courses have become more aware of and sensitive to the needs of international students and the strengths their diverse views bring to the university classroom. U.S. students who have interacted with our students have been exposed to new customs, traditions, and perspectives and have, we hope, broadened their world views (Worthen, 1991).

Of course, our IEP students have benefited significantly. By the time they are ready to matriculate, ELI students have been prepared for the transition to the university in numerous ways. Campus linkages woven throughout the curriculum have served as a strong motivating force, and students have known long in advance the linguistic and academic challenges they will face. As a result, their language learning has taken on new relevance in preparation for the rigors of full-time university work. In addition, they have become comfortable on campus. They have participated in a wide variety of actual or simulated university classes, have become familiar with campus facilities and procedures, and have formed relationships with students, professors, and other members of the university community. As a result, they are less likely to experience the culture shock that even U.S. students sometimes encounter when they enter a university classroom for the first time. With numerous strong ties to the campus, these students are much more likely to perform well academically.

Gee (1990) and others (e.g., Hicks, 1996) have pointed out that particular forms of discourse work to mediate the construction of knowledge in different communities. By achieving full membership in the academic discourse community, ELI students are empowered to participate in the knowledge construction process of their disciplines and contribute to it in significant ways.

❖ CONTRIBUTORS

Maria Dantas-Whitney is an instructor at the English Language Institute (ELI), Oregon State University, in the United States. Previously, she held several administrative positions in program coordination and student advising. She has also served as president of Oregon TESOL and chair of TESOL's IEP interest section. Her main areas of research are collaborative learning, content-based instruction, self-directed learning, and critical reflection. She is currently working on a PhD in teacher education.

Ann Lindsay Larson is an instructor at the English Language Institute (ELI), Oregon State University, in the United States. She has written and presented on the topics of individualized directed learning, academic preparation, content-based instruction, and critical thinking. She has developed the curriculum for several advanced-level courses at the ELI, including sheltered and adjunct university bridge courses. In 1994–1995, she taught in Poland.

Barbara Tolley Dowling is an instructor at the English Language Institute (ELI), Oregon State University, in the United States. She is coauthor of *Business Concepts for English Practice* (Heinle & Heinle, 1993) and coauthor of *University Survival Skills* (Newbury House, 1990). As a curriculum developer, she has been involved in planning and developing short-term ESP curricula and leading major change efforts at the ELI. Her main areas of interest are business English, self-directed learning, curriculum development, and organizational change. She has taught overseas in Great Britain, Mexico, Poland, and Thailand.

CHAPTER 4

One Intensive English Program's Approach to Preparing Students for Graduate Study in the Disciplines

Sarah Rilling

❖ INTRODUCTION

In many intensive English programs (IEPs) advanced English as a second language (ESL) writing courses prepare students to write research papers based predominantly on library and Internet research and personal experience (see, e.g., Moulton & Holmes, 2000). Skills associated with this type of writing include locating and reviewing historic and current research on a given topic and selecting, organizing, and presenting this information logically in an academic essay format. The assumption underlying such writing courses is that general English skills will transfer to other academic writing tasks. Academic preparation should, however, "go beyond the case where a general basic ESL course teaches a student some English with the result that the student can make some sense of any content course he takes later" (Mohan, cited in Brooks, 1988, p. 30). Whereas the basic writing skills we teach students in general ESL writing courses, such as synthesizing secondary library or Internet research materials, can transfer to writing tasks in the academic disciplines, graduate ESL students may additionally be asked to write the procedures and results of primary research conducted by the student. Students need adequate preparation for this type of writing task.

Some ESL programs prepare students to write original research results because many students, especially those preparing to study in graduate programs, need special writing skills to succeed academically as "written communication skills are essential in research success" (Sengupta, Forey, & Hamp-Lyons, 1999, p. S8). Graduate students may be required to conduct primary research in their graduate programs and write the results in the form of a thesis, dissertation, or professional paper with little guidance from their advisors on the form the writing should take (Dong, 1998). These students need specialized language skills prior to, or concurrent with, writing the thesis or dissertation. These skills include:

- defining and describing original research questions
- conducting efficient secondary literature searches in the library
- incorporating sources effectively without plagiarizing
- developing and describing research procedures
- describing the collection and analysis of data

- presenting research results
- describing implications of the findings

Students preparing to conduct independent research projects must learn the written conventions commonly used by experts in their own disciplines (Dudley-Evans, 1995). The organizational forms of academic writing have been described by many researchers in genre studies (see, e.g., Posteguillo on the organization of computer science research articles, 1999; Swales on the organization of research articles, 1990; and Zimmerman & Rodrigues on the organization of research papers in several disciplines, 1992). The language internal to specific sections of research reports has also been explored (e.g., Dudley-Evans on discussion sections, 1994; Swales on introductions, 1990). However, because such work is published in research-oriented publications, it may remain less accessible to practicing teachers (Hyon, 1996).

Although it is important to "make the learner aware of the structure and purpose of the texts of different genres, the significant features, and to empower him/her with the strategies necessary to replicate these features in his/her own production" (Kay & Dudley-Evans, 1998, p. 309), few classroom applications for teaching these strategies to ESL students have been described. Benson and Heidish (1995) focus on cultural conventions of text production in teaching technical writing "as a recursive and strategic process" (p. 322). Jacoby, Leech, and Holten (1995) describe using peers in the revision process of technical research papers. They further present applications for teaching how to write discussion sections of a research article that focus on writing as a process and on the linguistic choices that writers make. Cargill, Cadman, and McGowan (2001) present a negotiated, collaborative postgraduate writing program using intersecting genres from a variety of fields of study. This chapter adds to the growing number of essays applying theory to pedagogy in preparing students for the demands of writing and presenting their own research.

The Graduate Research and Writing course (GRW) prepares graduate students to present primary research (in oral and written forms) using a genre-based approach tailored to each student's respective discipline. The following section describes the course as fitting into the overall goals of the IEP at Colorado State University (CSU). The course itself is explained in detail with reference to different tasks for developing skills in reporting original research. Challenges of the course are discussed, including how students from a variety of disciplines and with a range of language abilities, can be served by a single course. Potential extensions of this course are discussed, including the use of computerized, corpus-based research for students to make discoveries about the language and organization of research papers in their own disciplines.

◈ CONTEXT

The Curriculum at CSU's IEP

CSU's IEP has courses at six levels, from beginning to advanced (see Colorado State University, 1999). Courses in all language skills (listening/speaking, reading/writing, and grammar) are taught at all levels, and elective courses (e.g., pronunciation, business and professional English) are taught at the advanced levels. Although instruction at the lower levels (basic, Levels 1 and 2) focuses on general language development, the more advanced courses (Levels 3, 4, and GRW) provide students with language skills necessary to compete in undergraduate and graduate study at English-speaking universities. Students at the basic, 1, and 2 levels study full time in the IEP, whereas students at Levels 3 and 4 may study part time at the IEP and part time at CSU. Students in GRW must be enrolled concurrently in at least one university course.

The IEP offers five regular terms per calendar year (7 weeks each) plus one 4-week intersession term during the late summer. GRW is the exception as it is a full-semester course, paralleling CSU's semester. Upon arrival, students are placed into a level based on performance on a battery of standardized and program-based tests. Diagnostic tasks are also completed early in each course in order to fine-tune placement. Though some students place into GRW, most come to the course having completed one or more terms in the IEP. Completion of the IEP depends on student performance in each class. Most students move smoothly from one level to the next.

GRW was developed at CSU's IEP in response to a need to prepare graduate students to read, write, and orally present research specific to their respective disciplines. Although reading and composition courses at Levels 3 and 4 in the IEP focus on general academic reading and writing skills, it was felt that graduate students needed specialized skills in presenting original research. During the several years it has been taught, GRW has evolved from an advanced-level course designed to teach general research and writing skills to the current, genre-based course, which focuses on writing conventions and organizational patterns specific to each student's discipline. GRW expands reading strategies taught in Levels 3 and 4 reading/composition courses, such as skimming, predicting from headlines (or headings) and graphic images, and using abstracts. Writing skills, including referencing outside texts, are also reinforced and further practiced.

IEP Students

Students from more than 25 countries study at CSU's IEP every year, including approximately 40% from countries in the Middle East, 45% from Asian countries, and 15% from other parts of the world. There are roughly equal numbers of men and women in the IEP. Forty-five percent of the population are undergraduate students and 55% graduates. Only a small percentage of students study at the IEP for language improvement only; most are preparing for university studies, either at CSU or other postsecondary institutions.

Students in GRW reflect the demographics of the general IEP population. All are graduate students conditionally or fully admitted to graduate programs in CSU academic departments. Of the 17 students enrolled in the course in the Fall of 1999, one male and one female participant were enrolled in graduate programs at the doctoral level; all other students in the course were at the master's level. The mean Test of English as a Foreign Language (TOEFL) score for the group was 507 (standard deviation = 54). One of the students was already fully admitted to his program of study; his purpose in taking GRW was self-motivated: to improve his writing skills for success in civil engineering. The other 16 students in the course were fulfilling requirements to complete IEP courses in order to be matriculated to their respective programs of study. Characteristics of these students are summarized in Table 1.

TABLE 1. CHARACTERISTICS OF FALL 1999 GRADUATE RESEARCH AND WRITING STUDENTS

Gender	Number of Participants	Countries Represented	Disciplines Represented	TOEFL Range
Male	10	Egypt, Japan, Korea, Kuwait, Saudi Arabia	civil, mechanical, and electrical engineering; economics; mathematics	mean score = 493 standard deviation = 49 minimum score = 410 maximum score = 557
Female	7	Korea, Kuwait, Saudi Arabia, Taiwan, Thailand, United Arab Emirates	English literature; environmental health; human nutrition; sociology; statistics; TESL/ TEFL	mean score = 526 standard deviation = 58 minimum score = 477 maximum score = 650

GRW students are either conditionally or fully admitted to graduate programs of study at CSU. For some CSU departments, matriculating conditionally admitted students to the graduate program depends upon two conditions: completion of all courses in the IEP, including GRW; and successful completion of entry-level courses within the individual department. Such departments include civil and mechanical engineering. Other departments, such as business and chemistry at CSU, require that conditionally admitted students complete the IEP courses, including GRW, as well as demonstrate general academic language skills through the TOEFL.

Students in GRW must have completed all other IEP courses, and they must be enrolled simultaneously in courses in their graduate programs at the university. Since there are few graduate courses offered during the summer, GRW is offered only during the regular academic year. Most GRW students have completed at least one term of IEP courses prior to taking GRW.

◈ DESCRIPTION

GRW is a non–credit-bearing, semester-long course that graduate-level students take concurrently with regular courses in various departments at CSU. Students meet for 3 hours per week over the course of the 15-week semester. Through course tasks and activities, students demonstrate proficiency in

- understanding standard components of an experimental research paper, including the abstract, introduction, literature review, methods, results, discussion, and references

- understanding the organizational structure of research papers and theses or dissertations in their own disciplines

- the use of databases and reference materials in the university library related to the student's field

- the ability to write a research proposal, which may ultimately be submitted as a thesis or dissertation proposal to professors in the major discipline

- the use of standard conventions and formats in research paper writing, including in-text citations, appropriate intertextual paraphrase, and the use of graphs or charts

- orally representing the individual research agenda using visual aids where appropriate

- recognizing academic plagiarism and how to avoid it

The textbook for the course, *Writing Up Research* (Weissberg & Buker, 1990), focuses on standard conventions in writing short experimental research reports. It divides the research paper into five sections

1. abstract

2. introduction

3. methods

4. results

5. discussion

The introduction is further broken down into five parts that parallel *moves*, as described by Swales (1990) and further described by Weissberg and Buker (1990):

1. describing the basic context for the study

2. reviewing relevant literature

3. identifying the research gap (problem that previous research has not solved)

4. establishing the purpose for the current study

5. demonstrating the importance of the current study to the field

Writing Up Research uses excerpts from authentic studies to show the form and function of each section of the standard research report. These studies represent a range of disciplines, from biology to engineering, although there seems to be a bias toward educational research articles. Each chapter presents two or more excerpts from specific sections of research articles to provide models for exploratory exercises, with students identifying different language features customarily used in the specific section. For example, in the chapter on the review of literature, verb tenses are examined in order to demonstrate patterns commonly used in citing previous literature. When information is put in a prominent position within a sentence, the simple present tense is used. When the previous researcher's name is in a prominent position, however, simple past tense is often used. In the chapter on reporting research methodology, the use of the passive voice is explored in order to demonstrate how researchers often create a depersonalized stance in describing research procedures. The excerpts and exercises provide the nonnative student with some general guidelines to follow in their own writing.

The research excerpts in *Writing Up Research* can be used in teaching how to paraphrase or use citations appropriately. For example, I devised practice writing tasks in which students needed to cite the research articles from the text in order to practice quoting or referring to previous studies appropriately. In this way, students practiced using quotes and paraphrasing with accurate citation conventions while using the research texts in the course textbook to their fullest.

A strength of *Writing Up Research* is the library tasks that appear in each chapter. The library assignments require students to locate research articles related to their topic of inquiry and to compare the language conventions used in these research articles with the language conventions presented by the textbook. This allows the student to focus on the texts he or she needs to succeed in the content-area courses and in research writing.

Required assignments for the course move the student toward the goal of completing a thesis or dissertation proposal for conducting primary research in the student's academic discipline. Writing is approached step by step, and revisions based on peer, instructor, and advisor feedback are an integral part of the process in developing the final product: the thesis or dissertation proposal. All assignments assist the student in moving toward this goal and include:

- a written description of the specific research questions to be explored in the thesis or dissertation

- a written introduction, which moves the reader from the general topic through previous research on the specific topic (review of literature) to the research gap and how the current study will fill this gap

- an annotated bibliography of research articles related to the student's research questions

- the research proposal incorporating the introduction with an extended literature review and the research questions to be addressed in the study

- a reference list that includes all sources cited in the proposal

Some students in the course are far enough along in their studies to include the following written reports, which, when combined with the above written components, complete the research proposal:

- a methodology section of the research proposal describing materials and procedures for conducting the study

- a preliminary results section explaining preliminary data analysis

- an abstract of the research agenda

In addition to the above listed written components, each student must demonstrate proficiency in orally presenting their research agendas. In the preliminary presentation, the students discuss the research area to be explored and define technical terminology or jargon with which the audience may not be familiar. In the second presentation, the students assume a specialist audience and present their research questions, provide a brief overview of previous research on this topic, and, if applicable, present their proposed methodology. Students further demonstrate proficiency using university library resources, including the on-line book catalogue, discipline-specific databases for locating research articles, and other reference resources, such as the discipline-specific reference librarian and dictionaries.

◈ DISTINGUISHING FEATURES

Genre-Based Study and Individualized Development of GRW Students

In GRW, students work on projects related to their own thesis or dissertation topic. Students gather relevant research from the library and theses or dissertations from their departmental advisors for rhetorical analysis. In this way, each student works on different materials in the course drawn from the disciplines.

Genre analysis assists in developing GRW students' awareness of the rhetorical strategies used by experts in their respective fields as "studying the genres of professional and disciplinary communication provides important information about the textual dynamics of discourse communities" (Berkenkotter & Huckin, 1995, p. 21), the discourse community being members of the students' own disciplines. Writing and presentation practices accepted by that community of scholars and practitioners (Hyland, 1997) are analyzed and practiced in GRW. A genre-based approach is "empowering and enabling, allowing students to make sense of the world around them and participate in it, and be more aware of writing as a tool that can be used and manipulated" (Kay & Dudley-Evans, 1998, p. 310), especially keeping in mind the conventions used by the discourse community.

Each student is given a model of the organizational structure in the outline format of research articles in his or her field (for computer and electrical engineering, see the structures described by Posteguillo, 1999; for humanities, social sciences, and civil and mechanical engineering, see the structures described by Zimmerman & Rodrigues, 1992). Students compare these overarching organizational schemata with the organizing principles of the articles and thesis or dissertation they are reading individually that are related to their own research topics. By making comparisons, students become more familiar with the organizational schemata used in their own disciplines.

Understanding of the internal structures of different sections of the research article is developed through readings and activities in the course textbook (Weissberg & Buker, 1990) and by examining a model of the introductory section of a research article modified from Swales (1990) and a model of the discussion section of a research article modified from Dudley-Evans (1994). Students compare the moves and structures presented by these researchers with the organizing principles and language use of the appropriate sections of the articles and theses that they are reading. Students are encouraged throughout the process to note similarities and differences between these models and the language they actually encounter in their disciplinary reading. By immersing students in their own subject matter, and by providing generalized models, students' consciousness of the form and function of the sections of the articles is raised (Sengupta, Forey, & Hamp-Lyons, 1999) and active participation in the disciplinary community of writers is fostered (Berkenkotter & Huckin, 1995).

Advisor Support

Throughout GRW, students are encouraged to meet with their academic advisors to develop research and writing plans. Academic advisors assist students in developing research questions and in selecting appropriate materials to read. In addition, advisors can provide students with theses or dissertations written by other graduate students in the department, and these can serve as models of written products for the students to understand better the scope of writing they must eventually produce as culminating projects in their graduate programs.

The Intricacies of Conducting Library Research

ESL students in advanced-level writing courses often comment that they are not given enough support in locating research texts, either in the library or through the Internet. Because individual readings are vital to participation in GRW, students practice locating appropriate background reading materials in the library and through the Internet, and they are given guidance in critically reviewing these sources as an aide to deciding which materials to read. Students are immersed in conducting secondary research of this nature throughout the course, predominantly by using the university library.

During the early weeks of GRW, students are oriented to the library in a three-stage process. First, students meet once as a class in the library, where a reference librarian walks them through (a) using the on-line card catalogue to find books and journal titles, and (b) using discipline-specific databases to locate research articles in the students' fields of study. The library at CSU is equipped with two classrooms in which the librarian can demonstrate research processes by controlling the student computers from a central computer terminal. Although this serves as a useful introduction, many students do not gain the hands-on practice they need to conduct independent searches. Therefore, the next two steps in this research orientation give students such practice.

During the second visit to the library, students work in pairs (preferably with another student from the same discipline) to explore the on-line card catalogue to locate books and to search specific databases for references to research articles on topics related to the students' areas of interest. In pairs, students further explore the connection between the database and the on-line card catalogue to discover whether the CSU library subscribes to the relevant journal. Once this is established, the pairs go to the library stacks to search for the specific journals and books that they identified through their search processes. If the library does not own the materials, the students are asked to request the materials through the library's interlibrary loan service. Each individual completes a library research proficiencies checklist with support from the peer.

Finally, students meet individually with the instructor in the library to show their proficiency by demonstrating a search on a book and then on journal articles. At this stage, the instructor can identify problems that the students are having and guide them to more efficient search strategies or more effective databases. Students unused to conducting library research in an academic environment in the United States need the support of this three-stage library research orientation.

Strategies in discerning the relevance to the student's actual research topic of a research article, book, or Web site located through the search process are covered in class. These strategies include reading the table of contents of the book and skimming selected chapters; reading the abstract of a research article; skimming the reference list of the article, book, or Web site to determine if the sources that the author drew on are works that the student can identify with the research topic; and identifying the source of the material (i.e., recognizing the name value of the author, journal, or publisher of the material).

Over-reliance on the Internet as a source of information for writing in other ESL writing courses seems to have convinced at least several recent students that all materials should be on-line. Given current copyright restrictions, this just is not the case. Even though the number of full-text articles and on-line journals is increasing, most academic research continues to be paper bound. GRW students, at least, need to be continually reminded that the Internet as a resource in academic research is still extremely limited and ephemeral.

Avoiding Plagiarism

Plagiarism is addressed explicitly in most U.S. universities' codes of student and faculty conduct, yet it is a cultural construct about which internationals may have different conceptions (Deckert, 1993). Students may feel that an idea has been expressed so well in an article that they may not wish to transform the text into their own, perhaps substandard, words (Leki & Carson, 1997). GRW attempts to systematically teach students how to avoid plagiarism in their academic and professional writing. First, using practice writing tasks with the research paper excerpts from *Writing Up Research* (Weissberg & Buker, 1990), the instructor models to students correct and incorrect forms of citation. Displaying student writing samples and the original short excerpts on an overhead projector, the instructor demonstrates to the class appropriate forms of citation (both quotes and paraphrase). Next, the annotated bibliography assignment stresses that students write the bibliographic citation and note down important findings of articles and book chapters they read using their own words and quotes with proper page references. The next step, incorporating these citations into the literature review section of the students' own research proposals, is also approached as an exercise in paraphrasing and quoting. The choice between quoting and paraphrasing lies within the rhetorical practices of the student's discipline, which the student has discovered through genre analysis. Citing sources appropriately is key to academic and scholarly success; doing so without plagiarizing is a skill that requires practice.

◈ PRACTICAL IDEAS

There are several challenges to teaching the GRW course as it is envisioned at CSU. The following points address the challenges I have faced in teaching this course and the practical ideas I devised to overcome them.

Teacher Content Knowledge

Familiarize Yourself With Student Research Areas

The first challenge I encountered in teaching GRW is that most students in the course are in fields of study with which I am only marginally familiar, such as civil or electrical engineering or environmental health. The students are conducting research in areas such as water and toxin transport in dual porous materials, efficiency in TCP/IP protocols for Internet networking, or the toxic results of mishandling farm pesticides. Because I do not fully understand the topics that students are researching, it would be natural to teach the course in such a way as to promote reports written for a lay audience. However, this would defeat one of the main purposes of the GRW course: assisting the students in writing their thesis or dissertation proposals for a specialist audience (the thesis/dissertation committee). My purpose as instructor of the course, therefore, is to assist the students in writing and presenting their research in such a way that it will be acceptable to academic specialists in their fields.

One way I overcome my ignorance of their research topics is by assigning students a preliminary oral presentation based on their research topic early in the semester. Because they are presenting their areas of research to a lay audience, they are required to explain technical jargon through the use of simple definitions and diagrams. The other students and I then have an opportunity to ask questions about their areas of research. As a result of these presentations, I gain fundamental understanding of their topics. When I am responding to their written work, I can therefore focus my attention as a reader on clarity of exposition, use of appropriate citation conventions, and other language-related issues that may arise. By requiring this initial oral presentation, my students are made responsible for enlightening me and their classmates on their research topics and on technical jargon from research in that field. Their written reports then can address a technical audience, making use of the appropriate discourse of the discipline.

Another way I familiarize myself with the topics my students are writing about is by skimming a couple of research articles on each topic, which students have located in the library and submitted with their research questions. One of my purposes in reviewing these articles is to assist the students in identifying the rhetorical conventions of their own disciplines; another purpose is for me to gain a working knowledge of how experts in their fields structure written arguments. By becoming more familiar with the rhetoric of the research area, I am better able to read my students' research proposals and provide them with meaningful feedback. Clearly, I do not understand all of the content of these articles, so this can be a tedious task; however, by listening closely to the content of their preliminary presentations and by skimming articles related to their research, I am better able to respond meaningfully to their written work.

Course Relevance

Encourage Students to Understand the Writing Conventions of Their Specific Disciplines

A second challenge is in making the course relevant to students in areas of study that do not require experimental research protocols, such as English literature or mathematics. These disciplines may not expect students to conduct experimental research such as is presented in the course textbook. For a literature major, for example, the goal of a master's paper may be to: (a) identify a thesis (or theme) for literary analysis, (b) synthesize previous research on the thesis, (c) clearly present original insights into the thesis based on knowledge of the author; the historical, social, and political context in which the author was writing; and literary theory, and (d) support the thesis with citations from literary works. By applying a genre-based approach to the analysis of writing in the students' fields of study, I encourage the students to become autonomous learners who can discern the functions and formats of their own discipline's writing conventions. In other words, students with majors not requiring experimental research designs still benefit from the course by exploring the rhetoric of writing in their own disciplines and applying that knowledge to their own writing. The literature major then, by analyzing articles and theses in her own discipline, can be assisted in defining for herself the appropriate organizing principles and language conventions used in writing in her field.

Accommodating All Students

Individualize Content: Challenge Students

A third challenge is in accommodating students with a broad range of language skills. The average TOEFL score for the Fall 1999 group was 507, with a great range in scores (the standard deviation was 54). GRW students have completed all courses in the IEP except GRW; however, this does not ensure a group with homogeneous language skills. The individualized nature of the content of the course has meant that students can work on different amounts of reading materials. Weaker students can be asked to read fewer articles or book chapters in their disciplines and instead focus more on using course textbooks from their university classes to develop general and technical terminology as well as content-specific applications. In addition, I work individually with students in writing conferences twice per semester and tailor my questions and writing suggestions to each student's individual language level, academic realities, and academic goals. In this way, I can challenge each student to continue to develop language and research skills at his or her level of ability.

A related issue is that of teaching students who were placed into GRW and students who have moved through other courses in the IEP. Students placing directly into the course may not necessarily have some of the academic skills built into other IEP courses, such as presenting original survey results to a class, or writing summaries and annotations. GRW is designed to solve this problem by providing a review of skills and strategies in a way that students who already understand the concept (such as effective paraphrasing) receive additional practice, and students new to the skill receive instruction and practice. More complex writing tasks may need reinforcement from previous IEP instruction, so although the concept may have been introduced in other IEP classes, students may not be able to productively use the skill. For example, synthesizing or contrasting different authors' views in coherent prose may have been introduced in other IEP writing courses, but these skills need continued practice through a course such as GRW.

Appropriate Research Topics

Allow Students to Choose Topics That Support Their Academic Progress

A final challenge is assisting students with their research and writing projects because the students are at different stages in their CSU programs. About three fourths of the students in GRW are in their first or second semesters of study at the university, whereas the other one fourth are in their third or fourth semesters. Students who are more advanced in their university programs have generally identified a topic of research for their thesis or dissertation, but students just beginning their graduate studies often have not. One solution to this problem is to allow students early in their graduate programs to focus their research in GRW on topics related to the courses they are taking rather than on their own thesis or dissertation research. In this way, the course serves more to support their progress in their university courses than to assist them in writing a thesis or dissertation proposal. Students further along in their studies can focus their research and writing efforts in the GRW class on beginning or continuing research and writing on their thesis or dissertation. The more advanced students can further serve as models of academic success to students just beginning their programs.

◈ CONCLUSION

The disciplinary writing course in the IEP at CSU assists students in becoming familiar with the organizational patterns and language conventions (including proper forms of citation) in their own academic disciplines. Through course activities, students gain expertise in conducting effective library searches, writing in forms acceptable to a specialist audience, using sources appropriately, and orally presenting their research to lay and specialist audiences.

In the future, I would like to incorporate tasks for students to conduct corpus-based research on the computer in order to facilitate text analysis. According to Flowerdew (1993), having students conduct research on a corpus of texts within their own disciplines can have the effect of "emphasizing the process of acquiring new genres, rather than the product" (p. 306). Both process and product of text production can be illuminated through computerized text analyses with a concordance program. First, student-identified articles would be scanned into computer-readable form and students would then make hands-on discoveries about these articles with a computerized concordance program designed to conduct lexical searches in large bodies of computerized texts. Students can explore the function of specific lexical items, such as the conjunctions *however* or *but*. From these simple searches, students can determine how frequently these structures are used and in what section of the research articles they appear. More advanced concordance programs can also do simple grammatical searches, such as on the use of simple past tense. This would enable students to explore whether claims made in the course textbook about verb tenses used in the review of literature are accurate or not for their disciplines. Finally, some concordance programs are now equipped to find collocational patterns (lexical phrases), groups of words that occur together. This feature could be used to determine whether certain verbs always occur with the noun *research* (e.g., the verb *conduct*) or whether specific words co-occur with certain technical terms (e.g., what co-occurs with *metal* and *alloy*). By allowing students to make discoveries like these based on real texts in their own disciplines, they would become more aware of discipline-specific written conventions and writing practices.

◈ CONTRIBUTOR

Sarah Rilling is assistant professor of English at Colorado State University, in Fort Collins, in the United States, where she teaches TESL preparation and ESL courses. She has taught TESL, ESL, and EFL in higher education in the United States and Japan. Her research interests include disciplinary writing, computers in language teaching, gender and language use, and classroom-based research.

PART 2

Creating Collaborative Partnerships

CHAPTER 5

Intensive English Program and MATESL Program Linkages: Creating a Symbiotic Relationship

Randi Reppen and Fredricka L. Stoller

◈ INTRODUCTION

The intensive English program (IEP) at Northern Arizona University (NAU), like most other IEPs, faces many ongoing challenges. Some challenges are instructional in nature, involving issues related to curriculum and course design, materials selection, and teacher development. Other challenges fall into more administrative domains and involve budgetary matters, the maintenance of technology resources, student advocacy, liaison with campus units, community outreach, and student recruitment. Because our program is distinct from other academic units on campus (in terms of students, faculty, and administrative structure), there is the ever-present challenge of sustaining positive program visibility and promoting the IEP among members of the larger academic community (see Jenks, 1997).

Another challenge that faces the program involves the maintenance of a mutually beneficial relationship with the English department, which houses the IEP, and the faculty and students of its Master's in Teaching English as a Second Language (MATESL) program. Unlike many IEPs, ours has a close working relationship with the English department and its MATESL program. Thus, the challenge we face does not entail nurturing open channels of communication or a simple interchange of ideas; rather, the challenge involves maintaining an evolving relationship that responds to the needs of both programs.

The IEP-MATESL relationship began on strong footing because the IEP was initially founded (in 1987) to serve two purposes: to serve the linguistic and academic needs of newly matriculated international students and to serve as a living laboratory for MATESL students. As a living laboratory (not in the clinical or purely experimental sense), the IEP provides MATESL students with opportunities to apply their graduate training and translate theory into practice. Over the years, we have worked diligently to fine-tune the relationship between the IEP and MATESL program so that the interchanges that occur between the two are mutually beneficial, for faculty and students alike. In this chapter, we focus on efforts that have been made to create the symbiotic relationship that exists between the two programs.

◈ CONTEXT

The IEP showcased in this chapter is at NAU, a comprehensive university located in Flagstaff, Arizona, in the United States. The IEP is housed in the English department, which is composed of approximately 40 full-time faculty representing the disciplinary areas of applied linguistics and TESL, creative writing, English education, literature, and rhetoric and composition. Eight of the 40 faculty members are in the applied linguistics/TESL area. The IEP director, a tenure-track faculty member in applied linguistics/TESL, reports to the chair of the English department.

The majority of students enrolled in the IEP are provisionally admitted international students who have met the university's academic entrance requirements but who need to improve their academic English before beginning regular university courses full time. Upon successful completion of their IEP studies, regular admission status (for undergraduate and graduate study) is automatically granted to the students. Student numbers are small, with no more than 30 full-time students enrolled in any given semester. Because of the small size of the program, the IEP has confined itself to English for academic purposes instruction at mid- to high-proficiency levels (see Stoller, 1999). Full-time IEP students are enrolled in 24 hours of classroom instruction per week.

The MATESL program enrolls graduate students with a variety of profiles: native and nonnative speakers of English (with TOEFL scores above 570); students with teaching experience and those with no previous teaching experience; international students from developed and developing countries; and students who want to teach at elementary, secondary, and tertiary levels in and outside the United States. All enroll in a combination of required courses (with emphases in linguistics and second language [L2] methodology) and electives.

All IEP instructors, except for the director (who also teaches in the program), are graduate teaching assistants (TAs), enrolled in our MATESL or PhD in applied linguistics programs. The IEP director supervises the TAs and oversees curricular decisions, course design, materials selection and development, and lesson planning. TAs are usually hired to teach in the IEP during the second year of their 2-year MATESL program. This rotation gives the maximum number of graduate students practical teaching experience. Although other IEPs might consider this shuffling of faculty to be problematic, we believe that the IEP and the MATESL program have benefited from this arrangement. It should be noted that this hiring policy emerged in response to our small IEP enrollments; if our IEP were larger, the ideal would be to hire increased numbers of graduate students for 2-year assistantships.

One of our greatest challenges has been devising an IEP curriculum that enriches the educational experiences of IEP students in addition to the graduate experiences of MATESL students, especially those who are not awarded teaching assistantships. Many curricular innovations that have emerged over the years have benefited IEP students as well as MATESL students. The MATESL curriculum has also evolved to take full advantage of the involvement of MATESL students in the IEP. The benefits of these curricular innovations and the innovations themselves are described in the next two sections of this chapter.

❖ DESCRIPTION

The establishment of formal, fluid, and complementary linkages between the IEP and MATESL program have always been a priority from the perspective of both programs. When our IEP was first established, few healthy IEP-MATESL partnerships existed to serve as models for a productive relationship between the two programs. Thus, we have spent the past 14 years developing a partnership that has helped the IEP and the MATESL program remain current and responsive to faculty and student needs in both programs. It should be noted that the linkages currently in place did not emerge mysteriously over time. Rather, they were carefully planned, implemented, evaluated, and perfected—through discussion, negotiation, and cooperation—by the IEP director and other MATESL faculty. Feedback solicited from MATESL students—from those with teaching assistantships and those without—has proven particularly useful in crafting meaningful connections between the two programs.

The impetus for a mutually beneficial IEP-MATESL relationship was straightforward in the early stages. When the IEP was founded, it was felt that an IEP association with a traditional, well-respected academic unit on campus would be important for the well-being, status, and longevity of the IEP. At the same time, the MATESL program was interested in providing graduate students practical teaching experiences and alternative forms of financial support. Equally important, both programs knew that the relationship had the potential for a dynamic and attractive blending of resources in response to complementary needs. Over time, a range of concrete linkages has developed, revealing additional benefits.

Benefits to the IEP

IEP students, faculty, and the program have benefited in many ways from their relationship with the MATESL program. Some of the most important benefits include the following:

- The IEP benefits from its close association with MATESL students, who are reading the most up-to-date literature and debating current issues in the field. MATESL students' fresh, and often unbiased, insights have led to curricular innovations, creative pedagogical techniques, and meaningful action research projects that have been reported at professional conferences (e.g., TESOL annual convention, regional NAFSA conference, AZ-TESOL affiliate conference) and in professional publications (e.g., Esposito, Marshall, & Stoller, 1997; Eyraud, Giles, Koenig, & Stoller, 2000; Herbert & Reppen, 1999; Mach & Stoller, 1997; Mach, Stoller, & Tardy, 1997; Stoller, White, & Wong, 1998). MATESL students, in a way, challenge the IEP to remain on the cutting edge of the field.

- Equally important are the easily accessible connections that the IEP has to MATESL faculty, who can contribute expertise in areas related to curriculum development, pedagogy, course design, materials development, and assessment. MATESL faculty involvement in the consideration and formulation of IEP policies and practices has benefited the IEP.

- IEP students benefit from a range of frequent in-class and out-of-class encounters with MATESL students (native and nonnative speakers of

English). These encounters, through, for example, our conversation partner program and intercultural communication class (described in the next section), serve important academic, social, and acculturation functions. Formal and informal interactions with MATESL students ensure maximum exposure to different speaking styles and registers. Furthermore, these connections assist IEP students in making a smoother transition into their new surroundings.

Benefits to the MATESL Program

Equally important outcomes from our IEP-MATESL linkages are the benefits to the MATESL program. Some of the most notable benefits include the following:

- The MATESL program, and its curriculum, can maintain a balance between theory and practice as a result of the IEP-MATESL association, thereby responding to the very real needs of MATESL students who are interacting with L2 learners from the start of their degree program.

- MATESL course content has new meaning for MATESL students when they see the relevance of key concepts (e.g., needs assessment, communicative competence, motivation, learner autonomy, interlanguage) and core knowledge (from, e.g., linguistics, sociolinguistics, L2 acquisition, methodology, curriculum design) in relation to IEP students and instruction. The hands-on experiences that MATESL students have with the IEP reinforce many topics covered in MATESL courses (see Grabe, Stoller, & Tardy, 2000). The insights that MATESL students take back to their graduate courses, after IEP encounters, enhance MATESL course discussions and class assignments, adding new dimensions to graduate training.

- MATESL faculty, knowing that their students will have opportunities throughout the degree program to translate theory into practice, can devise course projects and assignments that make use of real language learners and real language-classroom settings for real-world purposes, thereby bringing authenticity and realism to assigned tasks.

- MATESL students, as a result of IEP linkages with their degree program, have built-in opportunities to teach, tutor, observe classes, participate in select classes, conduct needs analyses, engage in research, and pilot teaching modules, stand-alone materials, and assessment measures. Exposure to many types of L2 learners and a range of teaching and learning encounters makes them more knowledgeable and, later on, more marketable.

- MATESL students serving as IEP TAs benefit from interactions with and support from the IEP director and other MATESL faculty. This built-in mentoring helps them gain confidence in addition to resources for future teaching situations.

◈ DISTINGUISHING FEATURES

As should be evident by now, our IEP and MATESL program are linked in numerous ways and at numerous levels. The IEP curriculum is specifically designed to involve

MATESL students, and MATESL classes are designed to build upon those experiences through special assignments, tasks, and discussions. All forms of MATESL student involvement in the IEP are considered integral to the MATESL graduate experience and, at the same time, critical for the integrity of the IEP curriculum. What seems to distinguish our IEP from many others is this active and purposeful integration of MATESL students into the IEP. Each form of involvement results in one or more of the following outcomes for MATESL students:

- credit hours toward graduation through TESL Practicum (an MATESL course)

- exposure to a range of teaching and learning environments

- social and/or multicultural encounters with nonnative speakers of English

- hands-on teaching experiences, with the support of a mentor

- completion of MATESL class projects with real students, in real classroom contexts

Below we describe seven major forms of MATESL student involvement in the IEP, each one representing a concrete connector between the two programs. We have divided these linkages into two main sections: linkages for which MATESL students earn practicum credit and those for which no formal academic credit is given. The few exceptions to this rule are noted in the discussion below.

Linkages for Which MATESL Students Earn Practicum Credit

In this section we describe four IEP-MATESL linkages for which MATESL students receive academic credit. As background, it is important to mention that MATESL students at NAU enroll in a one-credit TESL practicum each semester during their 2-year, 4-semester program of study. Students usually receive different practicum assignments each semester, involving hands-on experiences with L2 learners either in the IEP or the community. Described here are those assignments involving the IEP.

Teaching Assistantships

Probably the most conventional programmatic link between the IEP and MATESL program is the MATESL students' involvement in the IEP as TAs. Students in their second/final year of our MATESL program have the opportunity to teach in the IEP as TAs. Providing up to 8 hours of weekly instruction, they work closely with the IEP director and peer instructors to implement the EAP curriculum as well as innovate when appropriate. Because the TAs are in the final year of their graduate studies, they are eager to incorporate what they are learning in their MATESL courses into their teaching. This eagerness, coupled with the sound judgments of the IEP director, have led to a constantly evolving IEP curriculum. The combination of the director's mature professional perspectives and the fresh ideas of newcomers to the field has resulted in a vibrant teaching and learning environment. IEP students are not the sole beneficiaries of these combined efforts; MATESL students serving as TAs are beneficiaries, as well. The TAs gain valuable hands-on teaching experience and are given opportunities to pilot innovative ideas that they can present to future employers. Because a substantial portion of our curriculum is content based (approximately 50%), our IEP instructors gain valuable experience in an area that is becoming increasingly more common in L2 programs worldwide.

Tutorials

The second link between the IEP and MATESL program involves individualized tutorials in our IEP. MATESL students often spend 1 or 2 semesters earning practicum credit by providing individualized instruction to IEP students in language skills needing special attention (e.g., writing, pronunciation, speaking fluency, and reading rate). The IEP curriculum is structured to provide individualized tutorials, rather than whole class instruction, in particular aspects of language. The tutorials give IEP students personalized attention while simultaneously providing MATESL students with the opportunity to work one-on-one with a student and develop teaching skills and materials in a focused area of language instruction.

During a semester-long tutorial, MATESL students conduct an initial needs analysis and then, through ongoing assessment, determine the best direction for instruction. For the MATESL student, tutorials represent a nonthreatening introduction to multiple dimensions of teaching, with the support of the MATESL faculty member overseeing the Practicum and without the daunting task of planning instruction for an entire class. IEP students benefit from the focused instruction in an area of great need, allowing them to make progress at their own pace.

Conversation Partnerships

Another important IEP-MATESL link is the IEP's conversation partner program that pairs IEP students with MATESL students for a semester-long partnership. Typically an MATESL student will be assigned to a group of two or three IEP students, creating an ideal situation to practice many aspects of conversation (e.g., topic initiation, topic shift, interruptions). Conversation partner program participation is voluntary for IEP students; those who participate meet with their partners for 2 hours each week. The partnership is mutually beneficial. For the IEP student, the partnership provides opportunities for informal conversation and the chance to meet on a regular basis with someone familiar with the university environment and community. The partnership assists IEP students in adjusting to their new environment. In essence, the MATESL partner serves as a cultural liaison who not only provides the IEP student with a rich and safe environment in which to practice informal spoken English but also provides the IEP student with important cultural information (e.g., dealing with roommate conflicts, opening a bank account, participating in community activities).

For the MATESL student, the benefits of the partnership are equally valuable. While studying about L2 acquisition—in relation to, for example, interlanguage, pragmatics, language variation, speech acts, turn-taking, phonetics, and culture shock, MATESL students observe, firsthand, the trials and tribulations as well as the joys associated with mastering a new language and adapting to a new culture. For instance, MATESL students participating in the conversation partner program often witness the stages of culture shock that they have read about in textbooks or experienced in their own travels. When their IEP partners are experiencing the negative effects of culture shock, MATESL students can help them understand what is going on, thereby easing the impact of culture shock. The partnership also provides MATESL students with an easily accessible informant for MATESL course projects (e.g., a needs assessment project to determine an L2 learner's communicative competence). (See Stoller, Hodges, & Kimbrough, 1995, for details about the conversation partner program.)

Participation in the Intercultural Communication Course

The Intercultural Communication (IC) class, one component of the IEP curriculum, represents one of the most popular linkages between the IEP and MATESL program. The IC class is designed to provide IEP and MATESL students with the opportunity to participate as equals in a semester-long, student-centered class. Typically, five to eight MATESL students are assigned to the IC class. We make an effort to assign new international students in our MATESL program to this practicum option early in their program of study. Thus, we have native- and nonnative-English-speaking MATESL students participating in the class, alongside the IEP students. All participants, in the once-a-week 2-hour class, develop increased intercultural sensitivities and cross-linguistic awareness through a series of experiential cross-cultural and human-relations training activities. During class sessions, participants actively explore issues that are relevant to their immediate social and academic lives, including cultural adjustment, culture shock, stereotypes, the dynamics of verbal and nonverbal communication, culturally determined perceptions, conflict resolution, and values (see Weeks, Pederson, & Brislin, 1979). These activities, usually structured to include pair work and small-group discussion, help participants explore their own unstated, culturally determined values, and allow students to experience the logic of other culturally determined systems. As counterproductive stereotypes and preju-dices are examined, participants develop a more tolerant attitude toward people from other cultures. Because the topics oblige students to present views that at times contradict or challenge the belief systems of others, the IC facilitator establishes a congenial, nonthreatening atmosphere, which encourages participants to exchange differing, and perhaps opposing, viewpoints. To that end, the IC classroom is structured as a nontraditional classroom (with chairs in large or small circles), and with refreshments at break time (see Maggio & Gay, 1986).

IEP and MATESL students enrolled in IC are enthusiastic about the experience. Each session represents a valuable learning experience during which participants learn about one other and about themselves. Yet the benefits of the course span far beyond the content of the course. IEP students gain the additional benefit of having opportunities to speak in a relaxed atmosphere about topics that matter to them with a range of native and nativelike speakers of English; the result is increased confidence, motivation, and enhanced self-esteem. MATESL students gain the additional benefit of exposure to the mechanics of a student-centered classroom and the effective use of pairs, groups, and cooperative learning principles to maximize meaningful student-student interactions.

The IC class is structured so that each MATESL participant teaches at least one IC session. With the support of the IC instructor (a TA) and the IEP director, MATESL participants plan and implement a complete IC lesson. The mentoring that they receive builds their confidence and contributes to their teaching experience. By the end of the semester, all MATESL participants have taught at least 1 session and participated in 14 others, giving them access to 15 lessons that they can take with them and adapt to other teaching situations.

It should be noted that this special teaching arrangement offers special advantages to the IEP students in the class. The IC experience exposes IEP students to a range of teaching styles, a variety of English speakers in the role of teacher, and different classroom dynamics. This exposure, all within the confines of a safe and protective environment, prepares IEP students for some of the variation they will encounter in mainstream courses.

Linkages for Which MATESL Students Do Not Earn Practicum Credit

The three IEP-MATESL linkages described below are different from those in the previous section primarily because they are not associated with practicum credit hours. Despite this difference, MATESL students are enthusiastic about being involved in these IEP activities. Similarly, IEP students benefit from these linkages. For the MATESL students, these connections offer multiple advantages, including exposure to different aspects of L2 education, encounters with L2 learners in different settings, and opportunities to develop and pilot materials that are tailored to real student audiences. IEP students simultaneously benefit from the additional exposure to different speakers of English and the enthusiasm and energy of the MATESL students, who are planning special activities and workshops for them.

Special Academic and Nonacademic Activities

Another popular link between the IEP and MATESL program involves MATESL students in the planning and implementation of special academic and nonacademic activities that are not part of the standard IEP curriculum. Depending on the interests and expertise of the MATESL students, on the one hand, and the needs of IEP students in a given semester, on the other, MATESL students are invited to conduct customized workshops targeting areas of specific concern to IEP students. In past years, workshops have covered topics such as test-taking strategies, strategic reading, note-taking tips, writing research papers, and transitioning to major-specific university courses. Although these topics are covered in regular IEP courses, IEP students benefit from additional sessions dedicated to select aspects of larger topics. MATESL students gain experience planning a specific lesson, creating accompanying handouts, conducting the workshop, and evaluating outcomes. Workshop content is often directly linked to topics being covered in MATESL classes (e.g., reading strategies in a methodology course, article usage in the grammatical foundations course, test-taking strategies in the testing course).

In addition to these academic workshops, we are currently piloting a practicum option in which MATESL students plan one monthly nonacademic activity for IEP students (e.g., a movie night, a brown-bag lunch addressing a specific theme, elk watching, an outing to a local café, day hikes, a sports event). These activities provide a good platform for building friendships and create a variety of contexts for language interchange. IEP students benefit from the language exposure and practice, and MATESL students benefit from conversing with IEP students of different proficiency levels and language backgrounds. It should be noted that the idea of regularly scheduled activities emerged naturally from the IEP's attempt to address students' academic and nonacademic needs. The IEP has always hosted two informal events each semester to bring IEP and MATESL students together. During the first 6 weeks of the semester, the IEP director hosts a potluck (with the best food in town) for the IEP and MATESL students involved in the activities described in this chapter (for a total of about 50 people at the potluck). At the end of the semester, the IEP holds a luncheon or organizes a picnic to recognize the accomplishments of IEP students and to express appreciation to MATESL students who have given time and energy to the IEP. From the success of these events, IEP and MATESL students requested more informal opportunities to mix together, thus the creation of the once-a-month activities.

Guest Visits to IEP Classes

This vital link between the IEP and MATESL program involves guest visits by MATESL students to IEP classes. These guest visits have varied in purpose, though most involve guest lectures in the content-based component of the curriculum. During select thematic units, MATESL students who have expertise in the theme under investigation (e.g., art, archeology, plant identification, astronomy, Native American cultures) are invited to give guest lectures. These lectures are beneficial to MATESL and IEP students as well as to the IEP instructors. MATESL guest lecturers benefit from the opportunity to prepare and deliver a lecture to nonnative English speakers, and IEP students benefit from exposure to relevant content information and to another English speaker who may present information in a new way. IEP instructors benefit in that the thematic units they are developing are enhanced by the content information introduced by the guest speaker.

Guest visits from MATESL students include other configurations, as well. Most thematic units in the core content-based component of the IEP curriculum culminate with one or more major tasks, usually requiring IEP students to synthesize information from multiple sources. Culminating activities have included formal debates, panel discussions, science exhibits, simulations, oral presentations, and poster displays (as well as more standard research and synthesis papers). MATESL students are invited to attend many of these culminating activities, to serve as a real audience for IEP students and to witness state-of-the-art teaching practices. Although MATESL student attendance is not required, most attend these events to support their conversation partners, IC classmates, and MATESL peers who are teaching in the IEP. During culminating activities such as public debates, oral presentations, and panel discussions, MATESL students are encouraged to ask IEP students questions or to vote on the most persuasive debate team or best science project. Having a real audience, rather than just the teacher, creates a vibrant learning atmosphere for the IEP students. During poster sessions, MATESL students visit each poster display and converse with the student (or student group), once again serving as a real audience. The IEP students benefit from explaining their projects to uninformed viewers (unlike their instructors, who have seen the project through various stages and who, by the end, are quite familiar with the content). At the same time, MATESL students gain from witnessing L2 students grapple with language in challenging situations. In addition, it is hoped that MATESL students will take away with them a range of instructional ideas they can adapt to future teaching contexts.

MATESL Class Projects

The last IEP-MATESL linkage we would like to introduce relates to MATESL student class projects. Using IEP student needs, course objectives, and curricula to define project parameters, MATESL students often design and implement graduate class projects that involve the active participation of IEP students. Before embarking on their projects, MATESL students confer with the IEP director to get approval for their projects. This preliminary step protects IEP students and requires that MATESL students provide a rationale for their projects, explain the details of their projects, and describe the type of feedback they will provide to IEP participants. Most MATESL class projects are conducted out of class with IEP student volunteers. IEP students are usually eager to participate because of their level of familiarity with the MATESL students (as a result of other linkages) and the realization that these projects provide additional feedback on their English abilities.

Some examples of MATESL classes that regularly link with the IEP through class projects are listed below. What we include here is the formal name of the course and a sampling of projects that make use of IEP resources:

> ***Fundamentals of Second Language Teaching.*** MATESL students conduct needs analyses of IEP students, focusing on, for example, global needs, grammatical-rhetorical needs, sociolinguistic competence, and strategic competence (see Tarone & Yule, 1989).

> ***Assessment for Language Skills.*** MATESL students design assessment measures, targeting specific language skills or strategies, and administer them to IEP students. MATESL students analyze and interpret the results as well as evaluate their assessment instruments.

> ***Cross-Cultural Aspects of Language Learning.*** MATESL students design a tool for collecting cultural information from an IEP informant and then write a cultural ethnography.

> ***Sociolinguistics.*** MATESL students analyze classroom discourse (e.g., turn taking, teacher/student talk), explore pragmatic competence, or examine register variation through data collection in IEP classes.

> ***Second Language Acquisition.*** MATESL students design and conduct a study with one or more IEP students to examine aspects of L2 acquisition.

> ***Grammatical Foundations.*** MATESL students evaluate IEP students' written work to identify key grammatical problems.

> ***ESL Methodology.*** MATESL students design and deliver minilessons to IEP students, targeting a specific skill or strategy.

> ***ESL Curriculum and Program Administration.*** MATESL students develop instructional units and accompanying materials, with IEP objectives in mind, to be considered for future use or adaptation in the IEP.

The class projects described here, though just a subset, suggest a range of benefits for MATESL students, IEP students, and the IEP and MATESL program. MATESL students gain valuable experience as they prepare and implement materials for a real audience; the insights gained from the experience add to their professional knowledge base. IEP students have the opportunity to use language outside of class and receive individualized feedback. The IEP director and instructors benefit from increased insights about their students and access to materials that can be adapted for future IEP use. Moreover, the discussions that evolve from IEP director-MATESL student exchanges, during project development stages, are stimulating for everyone involved and positively impact the vitality of the IEP. Finally, the relevance of the projects, coupled with the insights and questions that emerge from MATESL student involvement, adds interesting dimensions to MATESL course discussions and the interpretation of course readings.

◈ PRACTICAL IDEAS

The IEP-MATESL program linkages outlined in this chapter represent carefully conceived responses to the context in which we find ourselves (e.g., IEP size, IEP student needs, IEP faculty experience, MATESL program objectives) and the desire of both programs to develop a mutually enhancing, mutually reinforcing symbiotic relationship. The fact that both programs showcased here are located in the same academic unit increases opportunities for interaction, negotiation, implementation, and evaluation of linkages. However, being in the same academic unit is not obligatory for a fruitful relationship. What is critical for forging meaningful connections between two (or more) programs is the recognition that the cooperating programs have much to offer each other and that linkages can improve the effectiveness and vitality of all programs involved. For IEPs wanting to create linkages, or improve linkages that already exist, we offer the following seven suggestions.

Establish Connections With Other Campus Units

Identify one or more academic units on campus that would benefit from linkages with the IEP while enhancing the effectiveness of the IEP. Logical units to make connections with could include education programs, ESL certification programs, MATESL programs, and communications departments. It is essential that an academic unit appreciates and respects what the IEP has to offer; simultaneously, the IEP must value the potential contributions that the other program offers to IEP students, faculty, and the program as a whole.

Open Honest Channels of Communication

Identify points of common interest and concern. Work toward understanding how connections between the two programs could be mutually beneficial.

Nurture a Nonthreatening Relationship

Because IEPs are often involved in turf battles (see Carkin, 1997) and struggles for legitimacy (see Jenks, 1997) on their campuses, it is important to create a relationship characterized by mutual respect and trust.

Allow for a Bidirectional Idea Flow

Proposals for linkages can originate in the IEP and academic program. In this chapter, there are examples of linkages that have originated in both programs. For example, the use of IEP students for MATESL class projects represents a direct outgrowth of a graduate curriculum dedicated to providing hands-on experiences for MATESL students. In this case, MATESL professors worked with the IEP director to create policies and procedures allowing the ethical use of IEP students for MATESL class projects. The conversation partner program, on the other hand, stemmed from the IEP's recognition of IEP students' social and academic needs.

Start Small

Pilot select linkages and evaluate their effectiveness. Consider the options presented in this chapter in light of the context in which you work. Which linkages would be easiest to manage initially? Which linkages would provide the greatest benefits to both programs? What adaptations would have to be made for the linkages to be effective? What other linkages could you establish?

Be Patient

Realize that mutually beneficial linkages take time to develop and fine-tune. With patience, programs begin to see the benefits that they offer each other. With time, new linkages become apparent; as linkages evolve, new forms of cooperation and interchange are discovered.

Be Prepared to Make Changes

As both programs evolve (e.g., in terms of student enrollments, student needs, curricular objectives, administrative structures), be prepared to make changes in already established articulations to maximize benefits for as many people as possible. In our case, many linkages currently in place were established in response to our relatively small IEP. When our IEP has larger student enrollments, we will need to make changes in current practices and consider new IEP-MATESL connections. For example, when our IEP is larger, we might consider using MATESL students as assistants in IEP classrooms to reduce the teacher-student ratio, provide IEP students with additional types of feedback and support, and give MATESL students more in-class experiences. Or we might staff a multimedia learning assistance center with MATESL students, facilitating valuable hands-on experiences for MATESL students and worthwhile individualized instruction for IEP students. When the need arises, we might establish relationships with other academic departments so that our advanced IEP students can audit or enroll in mainstream classes for a transition experience.

◈ CONCLUSION

In this chapter, we have highlighted a number of linkages that have been established between our IEP and MATESL program. The IEP-MATESL connections presented represent responses to the context in which both programs operate and to the needs of IEP and MATESL students alike. In all cases, the linkages have enhanced the effectiveness and integrity of both programs. In essence, the driving force behind the articulations described here is the desire for mutually beneficial connections and the symbiotic relationship that results from them.

The linkages outlined in this chapter can be characterized in many different ways. One way of describing them is by dividing them into two major categories: academic and social. The more academic linkages (e.g., teaching assistantships, tutorials, guest lectures, class projects) enhance the language education and academic preparation of IEP students as well as the graduate training and professional development of MATESL students. The social connections (e.g., the conversation partner program, special activities) assist IEP students in making the transition to a new cultural environment and help MATESL students develop a heightened understanding of L2 learners' affective needs and an appreciation for the cultures represented. Some linkages, like the IC class, can be seen as a merging of these two orientations, providing participants with both academic and social benefits.

We encourage other IEPs to build meaningful linkages with other academic units. Although the linkages may differ considerably from those presented here, owing to different programmatic needs and different institutional circumstances, the advantages associated with creating mutually beneficial connections are many. Carefully orchestrated articulations can add energy, vitality, and creativity to all programs involved, greatly enhancing the educational experiences of students and faculty alike.

❖ CONTRIBUTORS

Randi Reppen is assistant professor of English at Northern Arizona University (NAU), in Flagstaff, in the United States, where she teaches in the MATESL and PhD in Applied Linguistics programs. She is the director of NAU's Program in Intensive English. She has been actively involved in program administration and teaching ESL for more than 10 years.

Fredricka L. Stoller is associate professor of English at Northern Arizona University, where she teaches in the MATESL and PhD in Applied Linguistics programs. She is the founding director of NAU's Program in Intensive English. She has written about IEP-related issues in the *TESOL Journal*, *Applied Language Learning*, *Applied Linguistics*, and *English Teaching Forum*, and has coedited (with Mary Ann Christison) a volume on language program administration, entitled *A Handbook for Language Program Administrators* (Alta, 1997).

CHAPTER 6

A Dance Among Learners: Creating a Total Learning Environment

Jeanne Hind

◈ INTRODUCTION

An ESL student writes when describing an area of her language skills that she would like to develop, "I'd like to improve about my speaking because I don't have much confidence." It's a simple request, but one that an ESL teacher might find difficult to address in a class of 15 other international students working on listening and speaking skills in an intensive English program (IEP) setting with a limited number of weeks in which to cover a specified curriculum. What opportunities can be offered to this student to help build her confidence? How can this self-esteem and confidence work be built into an already crammed 9-week intensive program listening-speaking course?

Three weeks after writing about her desire, the student reflects on her learning experience based on a newly offered course in which she participated. She still feels she needs more confidence, but notes:

> First, I speak more smooth. . . . Second, I learn about the way to interrupt other people. In addition, I joined the conversation more frequently. . . . I learn to enjoy speaking English from my partners. They are so funny and they really let me try to speak English. Before I took this class, I had been afraid to speak English especially with native speaker because I know it's not good idea that mistake is shame thing even if I can learn so many things from mistakes. I couldn't try so much. Making mistakes cause successful. I can have more confidence than before. I'll try to speak English as far as I can.

Another student in the same class summed it up in this way, "I really enjoyed to be in class every time. . . . I could ask any question that I had without any shame. . . . This class was very helpful to improve my English." Another wrote simply, "My experience in this class was the best possible."

What type of setting had been created that made students feel so involved and that reflected so positively on their learning experiences? At the school where this course was offered, we call this a *total learning environment,* an environment in which all participants, both teachers and students, are constantly learning on some level.

The program, a combined partnership between an IEP and graduate courses in TESOL, was designed with the beliefs that learning is inevitable, that one cannot *not* learn (Clarke et al., 1998), and that learning is a socially situated process embedded in activity (Lave & Wenger, 1991). The best one can do as a teacher is to create activities for learning and join in the process. We nudge students along hoping that they will come away from the experience with new understandings, that they will have learned as we, the teachers have, from participation in the activity. In this setting, ESL students, graduate students (many of whom are teachers themselves), and teachers learn together. We are all learning and teaching something all the time.

IEPs and graduate programs in TESOL are often linked in some way. A partnership between a university department and an IEP located on its campus is not a unique idea. Involving graduate students in the IEP classes in various ways (e.g., as graduate teaching assistants, as interns, as tutors, as practicing teachers for a practicum requirement) is also not unusual. However, we believe that the model created at our institution represents a change from the more typical types of interactions IEPs and graduate programs have had. We have blended graduate study into IEP classrooms and created a total learning environment for everyone involved. We believe we have established a real community of learners.

This chapter describes one particular course that combines a graduate course on assessment and an IEP course. It looks at the way this partnership has created an exciting context for all participants—who have been asked to engage in a dance of learning.

◈ CONTEXT

Spring International Language Center (SILC), a privately owned institution, has been in partnership with the University of Colorado at Denver's School of Education since it was invited by the campus to start an IEP there in 1987. The campus is a consolidated urban model and houses three state institutions of higher education (a 2-year community college, a 4-year undergraduate college, and a university). SILC was invited to the campus to operate an IEP designed to serve all three institutions by preparing international students for entrance and academic success. The partnership with the university's School of Education is one of the linkages designed to benefit the students on campus.

SILC offers 9-week sessions, with 25 hours of language instruction per week. Six levels of language ability are offered, from beginning to advanced. Classes include a structural component integrated with a skills component (reading-writing and listening-speaking), plus elective courses. The elective courses may include modules designed to focus on specialized needs such as TOEFL preparation, conversation, pronunciation, vocabulary building, or on integrated language use through content.

From the time that SILC first opened its center, the School of Education's MA program in curriculum and instruction often used the program as a site for observation and teacher practical training. The relationship was one of cooperation: SILC cooperated by making its classes available for observation, and the university cooperated by recommending qualified graduate teaching assistants to practice teach at SILC. In this model of cooperation, the language school and the university retained separate identities because faculty members from each unit worked separately and focused on their individual students and courses. Interaction between the graduate students and SILC students was minimal during the observations. If the graduate students were asked to interact with the students, the focus was on the graduate students' assignment, which, ideally, fit in with something the ESL students would find useful. When the graduate student was working as a graduate teaching assistant (GTA), she or he became the teacher and the interaction was usually defined by the limits of the student-teacher role identities. The GTAs were typically graduate students with teaching experience who were assigned to teach one class during a term under the supervision of the center's assistant director. How this experience connected to their graduate work was not a focus for SILC. In other words, although we worked cooperatively, the connection between the learning of the SILC students, the SILC faculty, and the graduate students was not given much attention. SILC was simply a site used as a resource by the university's School of Education.

In 1996, faculty from SILC and the university began to talk about the partnership in different terms. The partnership then became a working relationship in which both partner schools worked together to define common goals which centered on problems of practice. Using Goodlad's (1994) four functions of partnership, we sought to accomplish through this joint activity

1. teacher preparation
2. professional development
3. curriculum and instruction renewal
4. inquiry and research

The relationship was to be one of collaboration with the focus of all activity on student learning, specifically on the ESL students learning English.

The challenge SILC faced as it entered this newly defined partnership was to ensure that the SILC faculty and students saw the graduate students and university faculty coming into our program as a resource we could utilize to improve SILC student learning. An unspoken concern was that the university faculty would come to our program with ideas of how we should be going about our practice and that the graduate students would use the SILC students to complete course assignments without really focusing on the learning of the students. However, we were able to overcome these challenges as we created a new model for cooperation.

In the summer of 1997, the two institutions established a joint institute known as the Rocky Mountain TESOL Institute (RMTI) with the goal of creating a total learning environment in which everyone involved in the institute, students and faculty, were learning on some scale. The institute sought to blur the lines between theory and practice through activities in which all learners were engaged. We argued that one did not build theory without practical knowledge and that one's teaching practice did not take place without some theoretical foundation or belief (Carr & Kemmis, 1986; Clandinin et al., 1993; Clarke et al.,1998; Cole & Knowles, 2000; Freeman, 1998). The ESL students would be seen as resources of knowledge for the graduate students to learn from as they reflected on their teaching practice and personal practical knowledge (Clandinin et al., 1993; Golombek, 1998). The graduate participants would be seen as resources of knowledge as they worked with the ESL students in activities aimed to improve the ESL learners' language skills. In addition, the SILC teachers and RMTI faculty would be engaged in professional development as we continued to explore personal, professional, and organizational change as the result of this challenge to our own personal assumptions about learning within the IEP context.

❖ DESCRIPTION

RMTI was created as an innovative exploration of English language teaching within the IEP setting. Its intention is to blur not only the lines between theory and practice, but also the roles we so often distinguish in education. Every participant in RMTI is both a learner and teacher, and each comes to the setting with a particular perspective.

In order to describe this program and its distinguishing features, however, we need to distinguish the participants in some way. Therefore, the learners whose primary focus is acquisition of English and who are enrolled in the SILC IEP are referred to as *SILC students*. The university graduate students, who are also teachers during the regular academic year, are referred to as *graduate participants*. The teachers in the SILC IEP are called *SILC teachers,* but some of them are also involved in the teaching of RMTI courses. The RMTI faculty (i.e., those who teach the graduate courses) are not an established body but rather a group of professional educators who at other times are identified as *teacher trainers, university or college professors, intensive English program teachers,* or *public school teachers.* This group of professionals, which changes in composition somewhat from year to year, comes together under the umbrella of RMTI to approach teacher education and ESL instruction in a new way. The institute is, therefore, a group made up of participants enrolled in graduate-level courses through RMTI, international students learning English at SILC, experienced ESL teachers teaching at SILC, and a faculty comprising teacher educators who wear other hats at other times. Everyone involved is also seen as a learner in RMTI. Each person in this total learning environment offers a valuable perspective to an understanding of learning and teaching.

The graduate participants in RMTI represent a wide variety of learners. Most are teachers. Many are public school teachers working on their MAs or ESL endorsement at the university; some are candidates in the newly designed TESOL certificate program; still others are teachers from countries outside the United States (native and nonnative speakers of English) who wish to add to their knowledge base through summer courses in the United States. A few people are exploring the field of ESL for the first time as they contemplate a career move.

The international students are all enrolled at SILC but they, too, have different reasons for studying at an IEP. Many have come to prepare for entrance into a U.S. college or university. The SILC program, which defines itself as an English for academic purposes program, was designed to serve this population. However, we also have students who are enrolled in university programs in their home country and who have come to the United States as a study abroad experience for a limited period of time. Still other SILC students are people who have come to learn English for reasons related to jobs or personal growth.

The SILC teachers all hold MAs in TESOL, applied linguistics, or education with a specialization in ESL. At SILC, professional development is seen as a part of one's practice as a teacher and learner. Teachers are valued for the insights they gain from their classrooms that lead to inquiry into improved teaching practices. An important aspect of RMTI is the involvement of the SILC teachers in RMTI courses. A few of the SILC teachers are part of the RMTI faculty, and either teach or coteach one of the RMTI courses. Other SILC teachers are involved in the institute as the teacher of a specific SILC class that is connected to a RMTI course.

Participant involvement depends on the model of collaboration being used in the RMTI course, which is agreed upon by both the SILC teacher and the RMTI faculty member. The model discussed in detail in this chapter is a module class, which offers complete integration between a short-term ESL class and a university course. Other models of collaboration include orchestrated participation, in which SILC teachers and RMTI faculty work together to create a gradual integration of language teaching activities and graduate course activities, and a teaching lab, in which graduate participants study a content or skill area and then observe and work with SILC students on that specific topic. Still other models include ESL students as experts and ESL teachers as experts, which feature activities such as panel discussions, presentations, or interviews with different experts.

The institute emphasizes a scholarship of practice. This requires teachers to examine their choices and the variables that influence those choices. A teacher brings to the classroom an awareness of language and learning acquired through study and personal classroom experience. The institute strives to bring these two strands of understanding into meaningful dialogue about teaching and learning.

The RMTI courses are held on site at SILC so that graduate participants, SILC students, SILC teachers and RMTI faculty are sharing the same space and involved in dialogue between classes. This increases the sense during the institute of a community of learners engaged in learning activities. Each RMTI course takes on a unique identity as the models of collaboration are determined and the activities in which all will engage are defined. What follows is a description of the institute and one course that illustrates the complex nature of a total learning environment.

❖ DISTINGUISHING FEATURES

What distinguishes RMTI and SILC course offerings from other more traditional models of cooperation between IEPs and graduate programs is the interaction between all students and the focus on the second language learner. Each RMTI course is linked to a SILC course or some aspect of the SILC organization. An overview of the courses offered through RMTI and their links to SILC classes is shown in Table 1.

Although each course and its link to SILC classes offers a particular case study of learning and innovation, the RMTI course and corresponding SILC class described here is one that I have taught for four summers. LLC 5055: Linking Assessment and Instruction is a required class in the university's MA in Curriculum and Instruction program. This graduate course is linked to a SILC module class called Focus on Language Skills. Course goals from each syllabus are shown in Figure 1 below.

Most graduate participants enroll in LLC 5055 with the expectation of coming away with some very practical answers to assessment dilemmas they may face in their own teaching settings. They are searching for best practices and clear guidelines on how to assess their second language learners, and they want answers. Typically, this class has an enrollment of 20–30 students and includes K–12 teachers (language arts, ESL, foreign language instruction, bilingual science and math, special education), IEP teachers, adult community ESL program teachers, EFL teachers from outside the United States, and individuals who hope to teach EFL.

During the 45-hour course, which takes place over a 3- or 4-week period, the

TABLE 1. RMTI COURSES AND THEIR LINKS TO SILC

University Course	Link to SILC classes	Model of Collaboration
LLC5030: Language and Literacy Acquisition I	Linked to listening and speaking classes	Orchestrated participation; ESL teachers as experts
LLC5055: Linking Assessment and Instruction in Language and Literacy, Part I	Linked to SILC module class: Focus on Language Skills	Module class; ESL students as experts
LLC5070: Linguistic Analysis of English: Implications for Teaching	Linked to SILC Grammar classes (all levels)	Orchestrated participation
LLC5820: Techniques for Teaching ESL	Linked to reading-writing classes (all levels)	Orchestrated participation; ESL teachers as experts
LLC5821: Phonology for TESOL	Linked to SILC pronunciation module classes: Basic Pronunciation and Accent Reduction	Teaching lab
LLC5835: Grammar Teaching Lab [prerequisite: LLC5070]	Linked to grammar classes (all levels)	Teaching lab
REM5080: Inquiry for teachers	Linked with SILC (faculty, classes and students) based on inquiry question	ESL teachers and students as experts

graduate participants develop a philosophy of assessment, create an assessment/literacy profile of a second language learner, create instructional materials based on assessment data collected on the learner, and develop a final assessment of their instruction. Approximately one third of the course time is spent working in teams (two or three graduate participants and one SILC student) on an assessment project. A final reflection piece is required in which participants are expected to consider what they learned over the course of their experiences in the class and in their interactions.

As part of the effort to blur lines between theory and practice, a structure was sought that would permit graduate education and teacher training to involve ESL learners in new ways. Thus, a particular feature of this course was designed, in which the SILC module course, Focus on Language Skills, would be part of a graduate course on assessment, and in turn the graduate course would be part of the SILC course. The SILC module is an entity in its own right as is the graduate course, but each relies on the presence of the other to work. The SILC course is offered as an elective class during the second half of a 9-week term. It meets over a 4-week period, with each class meeting 4.5 hours per week. Students who elect to enroll in this course are in our upper levels (Levels 4, 5, or 6), and the class enrollment is limited to approximately 10 students.

Course	Course Goals

LLC5055: Linking Assessment and Instruction	1. provide a forum for acquiring new ways, resources, and materials for assessing students
	
	2. explore personal beliefs about assessment recognizing often competing purposes of facilitating learning, assuring accountability, and evaluating student performance
	
	3. analyze and reflect upon assessment techniques to determine how our assessment practices link to our instruction
	
	4. develop assessment plans and articulate assessment decisions using a lab-type project with a learner
	
	5. complete the following tasks:
	  • philosophy of assessment
	  • team assessment project on your SILC student
	  • reflective piece on what you have learned about assessment based on work with the SILC student, your team, and the class

SILC: Focus on Language Skills	1. identify through self-assessment an area of your language learning that you wish to improve
	
	2. explore your learning styles and preferences by articulating these in a lab-type learning setting
	
	3. develop a learning relationship with a team of graduate students
	
	4. improve in your focus area through instruction, feedback, and practice sessions
	
	5. complete the following tasks:
	  • a self-assessment
	  • feedback logs on each meeting with the UCD team—what you did, what you learned, what worked, what didn't
	  • a summative reflective piece on your experience with the team

FIGURE 1. Course Goals

For the SILC students, the course offers an opportunity to work with proficient English speakers whose focus is to help them improve in an area of language ability they, the SILC students, have designated. For example, they might choose to work on areas such as idiomatic English, pronunciation, or writing skills. One student wrote, "I think this Focus on Language Skills class is a really good opportunity to talk with native speakers. I believe that talking with them make me have confidence in my speaking skill."

Some SILC students choose this course not because it offers an opportunity to improve on a skill area, but because it gives them a chance to interact with a native speaker. Some students change their initial expectations gradually. One student wrote, "At the first moment, when I was told about this class, I thought it would be boring, and I didn't want to take it. I decided to watch only a class, just give it a try." By the end of the course, he was able to write, "My experience in this class was the best possible."

Once enrolled in the course the SILC students need to complete a self-assessment and indicate what they want to learn. They are asked to consider this question: What does my team need to know so that they can help me improve in this area? They prepare information their team might find useful in assessing them (e.g., past placement scores, past TOEFL scores, samples of class work in the area they have chosen, suggestions on teachers to interview). For many, this is the first time they have thought about their own language learning in this way. They learn that they are experts of their own language knowledge and that what they know is useful to others who wish to work with them.

The self-assessment asks students to

- explain their purpose in studying
- assess their abilities in the four skill areas (reading, writing, listening, and speaking)
- choose one area for focus during the module and explain why it is important to them
- list their strengths and weaknesses in this skill area
- consider what they need to do to improve
- discuss what they have been doing to improve

The SILC students are also asked to keep a log and to cowrite a final reflection paper with the graduate participants in which they discuss their learning experiences. They describe their team members and explain the role they played in the decisions of the team. All other class assignments are determined by the team members. Prior to each team session, SILC students meet with their teacher for a debriefing period. They discuss the previous session with the graduate participants and share experiences with each other. It is during these debriefing periods that the teacher can suggest ways to offer feedback to the team or redirect the team effort.

The graduate participants meet the ESL students on their first day of the assessment course. They are thrown into an assessment predicament immediately. Because of the intensive nature of their graduate course, they must assess the students quickly, determine instructional exercises to fit their needs, and assess the instruction. This encounter forces them to bring together their theoretical and practical strands of knowledge and to begin to articulate their philosophy of assessment. The experience simulates what often happens to an ESL teacher who needs to begin instruction with very limited knowledge of the learner's language ability (Bailey, 1998). Graduate participants learn about the importance of individual learner differences, and they start to understand their dual role of learner and teacher.

As the faculty member for both the SILC module course and the graduate class, my role is to choreograph a dance between learners. Keeping the learning of the SILC students as the primary focus, I provide support and guidance to the graduate participants so that their work with the SILC students adds to their knowledge of assessment and allows them to make connections between theory and their own particular teaching setting. At the same time, I work with SILC students to help them see themselves as experts and to encourage them to take an active role in their own learning. I want all students in both courses to recognize that each has something to share; each is a necessary partner for the completion of a task.

I, too, am engaged in learning. During this class I work on articulating my philosophy of assessment and improving my practice and understanding of assessment issues. My pieces of writing undergo the same type of peer review in class as we share ideas and clarify thoughts. Teaching an assessment course offers me an opportunity to see if I do what I say I do. It is an inquiry project into my own practice of assessment. Over the past 4 years, I have noticed changes in my way of assessing the classes I teach. My own teaching practice undergoes constant change as I interact with the other institute participants as a teacher and a learner.

What makes this type of organized interaction (the total learning environment) lead to a sense of deeper commitment on the part of learners and a deeper understanding of the learning that takes place? I am convinced that it is not just the organizing of interactions between native and nonnative English speakers. Rather, it is the organizing of interactions that recognize the social nature of learning around activities in a community of practice (Lave & Wenger, 1991). If we define learning as change over time (Clarke et al., 1998) through participation in an activity; if we recognize that we learn apperceptively by "doing" together, then we can see why a structured learning opportunity like the one provided in RMTI works so well.

Evaluations for the module combined with the graduate course have been consistently and unanimously high for the ESL students and the graduate students. Each student found some aspect of the interaction valuable and each indicated that personal learning goals had been met. The following comments from course evaluations illustrate participants' perceptions.

For a SILC student, the chance for interaction was what stood out: "I think this class helped me a lot to improve my English and giving me more opportunity to talk to a native speaker made me more confident to speak in English."

For another it was the learning she discovered in the interaction:

I think that everyday, at any time, we can learn so many things that only depends on our desires to learn more and more. We can learn not only from school, but from our personal experiences and from the people we meet.

Another SILC student summed it up this way:

When this experience began, and I had the opportunity to meet my work team, I felt so comfortable because I perceived that they were much enthusiasm to do this work well. Soon, we had enough confidence to work together. . . . Now, when our experience together is almost done, I can say that it has been one of the most important things that I have made across all time I have been studying at Spring International. Mainly, because this experience has given to me the opportunity to establish direct contact with American people, and to work hard with them making a focus on areas where I need to work.

For the graduate participants, the experience was also very positive. They considered the activities and interactions essential to their grasp of complex assessment issues. Some expressed initial concern about working with a real language learner. One wrote, "I was not aware that so much emphasis would be placed on working with the ESL student. . . . I thought 'How am I going to be able to do this?' I am a teacher, but I teach ESL to elementary students." This student ended by saying that the experience changed the way she perceived assessment and related assessment to instruction.

Another graduate student summed up her experience this way:

> I really learned more about myself as a learner and as a teacher. I also refined my own belief system and added to my assessment philosophy. This class made me excited to "try out" new assessment techniques with my students in the fall.

One who does not work with ESL students on a regular basis noted that the work with the SILC students, "made this class a real experience and one I probably wouldn't otherwise have had the opportunity to experience." What made the interactions during this class seem so beneficial to the learners? My belief is that it is in the nature of the activities in which they were involved.

During the class both SILC students and graduate participants had learning goals; both were trying to derive benefit from the interaction. The graduate participants were not just teachers trying to help the ESL students learn English, they were also fellow students working on a class project; they were colleagues in learning. The SILC students were not just there to improve their language skills, they were experts in language learning who had something to share with the graduate participants. I was not just there to orchestrate this participation, but also to explore my own views on assessment. As I was asked questions, I was forced to rearticulate my own approach to assessment. I found I had an audience of experts with differing experiences who could offer me new insights. This balancing of learning and teaching distinguishes these interactions from more traditional interactions among IEP students, graduate students, and their instructor.

◈ PRACTICAL IDEAS

Putting together a partnership requires more than a handshake or a signed memorandum of understanding. Listed below are some important points to consider in designing a partnership of this type.

Create a Mutually Beneficial Partnership

Make sure you define the partnership between the university and the IEP as a two-way relationship in which both sides are viewed as experts and both have something to learn from the experience. Everyone involved in the activity becomes a learner on some level.

Be Flexible

Make the relationship flexible and dynamic. In other words, do not stay with one model of interaction and ignore others. Do not get caught up in defined roles and titles and miss some important opportunities for learning. As you build links and create models, adjustments will have to be made. Do not imagine that your initial blueprint will remain intact as the partnership evolves.

Remain Learner Focused

At all times, remember that the focus is on the learner. Avoid falling back into traditional relationships represented by dichotomies such as researcher (university-side)-informant (IEP-side) or professor (scholarly, theoretical)-teacher (practical). Always keep the focus on the learner and recognize that everyone involved is learning on some level. If all conversations, activities, and decisions are made around the ESL learner, many tensions can be avoided.

Keep Communication Channels Open

Include all parties involved in the conversation in the planning stages. This is simply a reminder that all involved need a voice and should be heard from at appropriate times prior to final decisions. Allow for ongoing feedback from all participants.

Construct a Community of Learners

Construct opportunities for the learning community to come together and share what they are learning so that a community of learners is created. Because food is always a great organizer, breakfast chats, brown bag lunches, and social events allow for successful interactions. Sometimes a crescendo event at the end of a class can add a wonderful sense of community while putting what has been learned into perspective.

◈ CONCLUSION

Creating this type of partnership requires that the programs involved focus on the language learner. The graduate program has to reconceptualize how teaching experiences are brought into teacher preparation. As Clarke et al. (1998) remind us, "The particulars of teaching must be understood in relationship to the multiple contexts within which they occur" (p. 595). An experience that requires active learning from all participants allows graduate students to understand these multiple contexts more clearly.

Just like the graduate program, the IEP community also undergoes a change. IEP teachers are asked to rethink how they frame student learning. They engage in ongoing professional development, as they question, reflect and learn from each other. They begin to see colleagues in new ways as they participate on panels, learn about their practice through graduate participant research, and take part in new conversations about teaching in the staff room. The utilization of graduate students and the creation of joint learning experiences heightens student learning as well as faculty professional development. The graduate students are not seen as intrusions, but as exciting additions to the learning community. Any difficulty becomes a potential learning point. The ESL students also begin to see themselves in new ways as they reflect on their learning experiences and serve as expert informants to other team members. The IEP administrator benefits as well because this type of activity allows one to take a new look at the program as it functions as a whole.

Once the learning community has a sense of self, the labels distinguishing its participants (ESL learner, graduate participant, university faculty, IEP faculty/administrator) begin to hold less importance to the relationship. This is an indication that a total learning environment has been created, whose members join together in a synchronized dance of learning.

◈ CONTRIBUTOR

Jeanne E. Hind is director of Spring International Language Center, on the Auraria Higher Education Center campus in Denver, Colorado, in the United States. She teaches an assessment class for the Rocky Mountain TESOL Institute and is a doctoral student at the University of Colorado at Denver, studying educational leadership and innovation.

CHAPTER 7

The Convergence of Experience and Emerging Pedagogy in the Creation of an Intensive English Program

Patricia Miller and JoAnn Crandall

◈ INTRODUCTION

This chapter offers an in-depth look at a U.S. government-funded international intensive English program (IEP) established by the Center for Applied Linguistics (CAL) in Honduras. CAL, working as the subcontractor with the Academy for Educational Development (AED), responded to a Request for Proposal issued by the United States Agency for International Development (USAID) mission in Honduras to prepare 430 Peace Scholars over a 4-year period for bachelor's degree study in the United States. The AED-CAL proposal was awarded the contract. CAL, as the language specialist, was responsible for designing and implementing the English and academic preparatory training in Honduras and the follow-on training in the United States; AED was responsible for the overall program, including orientation, placement, monitoring of the scholars in U.S. universities, and follow-up upon return.

Consequently, CAL established an IEP center in Tegucigalpa, the capital of Honduras, that provided 900 hours of English language training and 360 hours of academic content preparation over a 9-month period. This was followed by an additional 3 months of intensive English for academic purposes (EAP) classes in Washington DC, for a total of 1,500 hours of training. The IEP, which was called *CAPS*, after the Central American Peace Scholarship Project that funded it, was an integrated program of English and content that employed nine full-time English and nine part-time content teachers to teach approximately 110 students a year for 4 years.

Four Challenges

From the beginning, we (Patricia Miller, in Honduras, and JoAnn Crandall, in Washington, DC), as the IEP program directors, set out to create a learning environment that would meet the needs of the students. This was a challenge because the CAPS project targeted economically and socially disadvantaged high school graduates from rural environments who had had limited opportunity to develop the English proficiency or academic skills that would be needed in a U.S. university. For example, we knew their Test of English as a Foreign Language (TOEFL) scores would be lower than those required at most U.S. universities.

Consequently, our end-of-program targets were TOEFL scores of 450–500 for the in-country training and 550 after the 3 months of training in the United States.

Our second challenge was that there were few models to follow to prepare students such as these; we had only our theories, practices, and experience or intuition. In retrospect, we made sense of our experiences (Johnson, 1996), applied what we learned to current and emerging theory, and created a learning environment in which the students excelled.

The third challenge was professional development for the English and content teachers. This included learner-centered instruction, learning strategies, critical thinking, and ways to integrate language and content. Professional development for the English teachers also included review of practical classroom activities in each of the skill areas. Underlying the theories of learning and practical techniques was the philosophy of building the confidence and self-esteem of the students.

The fourth challenge was to build a team of committed teachers out of a culturally, linguistically, and academically diverse group. We needed teachers who were not only committed to their subject matter but also to the students and the program. During its 4-year existence, the program met its goals and sent the quota of 430 peace scholars to study in U.S. universities.

This case study describes in detail the context of the CAPS Project of the mid-1980s and the special IEP that created a culture that resulted in the acculturation of teachers and students to the program and assured future student acculturation to the rigorous academic demands of U.S. university study.

Keeping in mind acculturation to the program and academic life as the distinguishing features of the program, this chapter examines the learning theory, practice, and rationale that guided the program. Included in the discussion are academic language proficiency (Cummins, 1979), the integration of language and content (Crandall, 1987), the importance of initial cognitive learning in the first language (L1) (Cummins, 1979; Lambert & Tucker, 1972;), and the importance of developing responsibility and autonomy through active student learning and explicit application of learning strategies (Rubin & Thompson, 1982). For teachers, acculturation includes involvement in and commitment to the program as well as new approaches to program management and professional development. From this experience, we draw some practical ideas that encourage effective learning, which can be adapted to other learning contexts. Although some of these ideas are not surprising today, in the mid-1980s they were quite new.

◈ CONTEXT

The CAPS IEP was established in 1986. Its creation was directly connected to the political climate of the time, wherein the United States was increasing its support for international participant training, especially in Central and South America. The United States increased its economic assistance to Central America in part through the CAPS Project, which was intended to enable rural youth to be sent to the United States for undergraduate study in fields deemed appropriate by Central American government officials and USAID country representatives. Although governed by general core guidelines, the CAPS Project was configured and administered separately in each Central American country. Those individuals selected to be trained were called *Peace Scholars,* serving as mini-ambassadors from their countries while studying in the United States and returning to their countries to assume positions of leadership.

The USAID criteria stipulated that the scholarships be awarded to economically and socially disadvantaged individuals. Therefore, priority was given to recruiting young males and females from the Honduran rural and agricultural sector. Although all the students selected had completed secondary school, the schools they had attended had not provided the mathematics or science backgrounds expected in U.S. universities. In addition, few students had sufficient academic background in their L1 or English language proficiency to prepare them for U.S. academic study. They did, however, demonstrate educational and leadership potential. Approximately two thirds of the students were male. Their ages ranged from 20 to 39, with the majority under 30. Thus, most had been out of high school for at least 5 years. Few had been to the capital, Tegucigalpa, and even fewer had traveled outside of Honduras. Consequently, acculturation was an important theme.

Previously, CAL had undertaken a needs analysis for USAID to determine the feasibility of conducting English language training and academic preparation in the Central American countries. Both of us participated in that evaluation, the results of which demonstrated that there were institutions within these countries that could partner with U.S. institutions to conduct the training.

At this point, each USAID country office worked closely with host country government officials to decide on the configuration of its scholarship program, including the numbers of individuals to be trained and the amount and type of in-country training to provide. Each office issued a call for proposals to design and carry out the project from institutional, private, or a consortium of contractors. The USAID Office in Honduras selected AED as the prime contractor, with CAL as the subcontractor, in charge of education and training.

Consequently, CAL established a training center, developed a tentative program (which was continuously refined), and welcomed the first 110 students, who were selected based on their potential to be among the best and brightest in their country.

◈ DESCRIPTION

The CAPS program consisted of three 12-week cycles in Honduras, comprising 900 hours of English and 360 hours of content, complemented by another 300-hour cycle of EAP in the United States, for a total of more than 1,500 training hours over the course of a year.

The program design called for the development of English skills while students were also developing academic skills in Spanish, with increasing amounts of English added in each cycle until the program was delivered completely in English, beginning with the third cycle. Figure 1 outlines the program course components, course time, the language or academic skill emphasized, and the language spoken in class.

Cycle I, consisted of 5 hours of beginning English, with an emphasis on listening, reading, and controlled writing, and 2 hours of Spanish, with a focus on reading skills, literature, grammar, critical thinking skills, learning strategies, and writing. End-of-cycle TOEFL scores for this level ranged from 375–425.

Cycle II consisted of 5 hours of low intermediate-level English, emphasizing intensive reading and automaticity, listening, and paragraph writing, with 1 hour of either basic or intermediate-level math (the latter consisting of algebra and geometry) and 1 hour of basic science (focusing on basic biology). The math and science courses were taught bilingually, with a focus on the specific English of math and science. TOEFL scores at the end of this cycle ranged from 425–450.

Cycle III consisted of 5 hours of high intermediate-level English, with a beginning focus on EAP, 1 hour of calculus, and 1 hour of either advanced biology or physics, with the academic courses taught predominantly in English. The content focus for this cycle was a research paper taught collaboratively by the English and science teachers. TOEFL scores at the end of the 9-month in-country training program ranged from 450–500.

Cycle IV, taking place in the United States, again consisted of 5 hours daily of English, with an intensive EAP focus, and acculturation by exploring Washington DC. For the entire 1,500-hour program, end-of-course TOEFL scores ranged from 500–600, the majority of which were 550 or higher.

The program employed nine full-time English teachers with experience teaching English to adults and nine part-time math, science, and Spanish teachers who were university professors, some with PhD degrees. All but one of the teachers were bilingual; the English and content teachers included both L1 English and L1 Spanish speakers. The teachers were hired based on their credentials, experience, bilingual ability, experience in the United States (especially in the university environment), and personal interest, which included commitment to the program, commitment to excellence in teaching, a desire to learn, agreement with the objectives of CAPS, and perceived professionalism.

The CAPS IEP was an integrated program with four principal components. The most outstanding feature was the integration of academic English and content courses, with initial language concentration in the native language. The second component was the creation of a Learning Resource Center specifically designed to promote student responsibility and autonomy. The third feature was the inclusion of an intercultural component that emphasized Honduran culture and prepared students for the differences they would encounter in the United States. The last component was the incorporation of English acquisition activities designed to provide opportunities for the students to use English outside of the classroom and to promote camaraderie and cohesiveness.

With the need for student acculturation to the program and ultimately U.S. academic and social life, the entire program was designed to prepare the students academically, culturally, and personally. This student acculturation could not be accomplished without the acculturation of the teachers to the program. Consequently, student and teacher acculturation and team building were critical.

◈ DISTINGUISHING FEATURES

The Acculturation of Teachers and Students to the CAPS IEP

Considering the nature of our participants as well as the diverse characteristics of the teachers, we knew that the success of the program would be closely tied to how well the teachers and participants identified with its values and educational process.

Program Cycle (12 Weeks Each)	Course Component	Course Time	Language and/or Academic Skill Emphasized*	Language(s)
Cycle I	English	5 hours	Listening, reading, controlled writing, speaking	Predominately English; bilingual teachers used Spanish when necessary
	Spanish	2 hours	Reading, grammar, learning strategies, study skills, process writing, and critical thinking	All Spanish
Cycle II	English	5 hours	Reading, writing, listening, paragraph writing, speaking, math and science lexical and syntactic registers	All English
	Basic math	1 hour	Review of pre-algebra and algebra: word problems	Texts in English; discussion bilingual
	Science	1 hour	Review of basic biology: scientific method	Texts in English; discussion bilingual
Cycle III	English	5 hours	EAP discourse: reading, writing, listening, and speaking; oral fluency	All English
	Advanced math	1 hour	Introduction to calculus: basic problem solving	All English
	Advanced science	1 hour	Advanced biology or physics and chemistry; advanced problem solving: conducting research, writing research paper	All English

*All four skills were taught in each cycle, though the emphasis changed.

FIGURE 1. CAPS: The Integration of Language and Content

Consequently, as we designed the IEP curriculum and activities, we incorporated factors that would contribute to a climate ripe for learning and development: the acculturation of teachers and students to the program.

Teacher Acculturation

Teacher acculturation to the program, or team building and program commitment, was a prime consideration during program design. Five aspects were considered important:

1. a thorough program orientation that considered Honduran and USAID government perspectives, explained program design and rationale, and

      discussed Honduran-U.S. intercultural communication practices and educational traditions

2. the articulation of a CAPS educational program philosophy created by all the CAPS teachers

3. meaningful professional development activities that emerged from teacher perspectives on program needs, including program time for informal discussion and reflection on problems and solutions

4. a collaborative management orientation based on Peters and Waterman's (1982) *In Search of Excellence*

5. social activities that provided opportunities for teachers to get to know one another

Of special significance was the CAPS program management style (growing out of Peters & Waterman), the creation of the program philosophy by the teachers, and the professional development program.

Management Principles for Excellence

In Search of Excellence presents a series of case studies of the most successful companies in the United States. Throughout the case studies, a set of principles emerges, four of which we applied specifically to the CAPS program. We borrowed the overall theme of excellence, which was enthusiastically adopted by students and teachers. Excellence does not mean perfection, but rather individuals' use of resources to develop their potential over time. Those principles that fit our situation were: (a) close to the customer; (b) productivity through people; (c) hands on, value driven; and (d) simultaneous loose-tight properties.

Close to the Customer

The principle of being close to the customer concerns knowing students' needs and desires and meeting them. Moreover, being close to the customer means exactly that—being available to students and understanding them through the use of student needs assessments and inventories that help make teaching relevant to students' needs and experience. Every student was regarded as capable of success, and the environment emphasized a sense of caring for students.

Productivity Through People

The principle of productivity through people underscores creating the awareness in all teachers that their best efforts are important and that they will share in "the rewards of company success" (Peters & Waterman, 1982, p. i). This idea translated into considerable attention and contact with the teachers by program administration. In addition to informal chats, attention included observation, collaborative feedback, and follow up.

    To recognize teacher dedication and ideas, a merit system was established that included a series of financial and professional development incentives. Significant contributions to the program, the design of learning activities, and exemplary attendance were all recognized. Teachers nominated and evaluated their colleagues according to jointly agreed criteria. For example, one award went to a science teacher for her questions instantiating critical thinking. She later turned the topic into a professional development workshop on how to promote critical thinking. Another teacher was recognized for her special contribution to the program through her weekly student open house. A number of teachers also received recognition for their work in materials development, including the use of authentic reading materials.

Hands On, Value Driven

The principle of hands on, value driven expresses the need for a sound set of beliefs on which to base policies and actions as well as the need for people to find common ground with each other. The value-shaping manager is an implementer who directly instills values through deeds. Inherent in this principle is that all people in the program are important, education thrives in a climate of care, high student expectations and motivation must be maintained, learning and teaching need different styles, and learning thrives within a structure. How do you demonstrate that all people are important? We believed that you could do it by listening and talking with them, listening to their opinions, and considering their ideas.

Simultaneous Loose-Tight Properties

The idea of some central control existing simultaneously with autonomous and innovative teachers is expressed in the principle of simultaneous loose-tight properties. The CAPS program took seriously its commitment to excellence. We agreed on a core of principles and practices based on theory and experience that would facilitate learning. In addition, we also valued innovation, and each teacher had the freedom to discover, create, and utilize practices that he or she had found successful.

Teacher-Developed Program Philosophy

Not only did we want the teachers to believe they had a voice in designing the program, we wanted their ideas. Consequently, during the orientation before the program began, and after the presentations and discussions on U.S. and Honduran educational traditions, we began the process of establishing our program philosophy. Each teacher reflected on his or her most important educational values. Then we put all the values together, eliminating redundancies, distributed the list, and reflected on the values in light of our students. After several weeks of teaching, when we had a sense of the students, we met and agreed upon a final set of educational values and professional expectations. Figure 2 shows the CAPS program philosophy.

Professional Development

The professional development component consisted of one intensive 2-week phase of a preservice program, followed by regular weekly in-service sessions and 2-day end-of-cycle workshops.

The preservice program was conducted together with the total program orientation and began from the context of Honduran and U.S. educational traditions. General preservice included the following eight components:

1. theory of language acquisition
2. learner characteristics, including individual styles
3. classroom management

1. We believe that education should promote the growth of the individual. Consequently, we need to motivate our students toward responsibility, independence, and initiative. This includes the students? responsibility for his or her own work and learning. Peer and self-assessment are core skills in the growth of the individual.

2. We believe that education thrives in a climate of discipline and care. Learning proceeds from love with attention to high standards.

3. We believe that teaching does not presume any single strategy, that a variety of teaching strategies should be used to meet the different learning styles of our students.

4. We believe that education should be life-related, that it should teach meaning on a profound level, with the social skills necessary to function as a productive citizen. The concept of cooperation is essential to productive community life.

5. We do not presume to know all the answers. We believe we can learn from our students just as they learn from us.

6. We recognize that all our students are different and that they are at different stages of learning and English language acquisition. In order to provide quality education, we teach to individual needs, rather than general needs. Whenever we can, we individualize and personalize learning.

7. We believe that in our particular program, everything we do is part of a larger concept. We operate on the basis of a system approach. We use our resources in efficient ways so that our objectives are met as expected.

8. We believe that learning transpires in a positive affective environment (Krashen, 1980, 1982, 1985) characterized by optimism, flexibility, and open-mindedness. In a positive environment, negativism, complaining, condemning, or gossiping are out of place and can undermine learning.

9. We believe that we motivate our students toward excellence by serving as models: through our own enthusiasm, our passion for teaching, and our love for learning.

10. Finally, we believe the teaching of math and science should present the scientific and mathematical concepts in a way that they can be related to everyday life.

As teachers in the CAPS program, we believe that our exemplary personal conduct facilitates the learning environment; we serve as models for our students.

1. We are responsible: That is, we are cooperative, organized, and punctual.

2. We demonstrate integrity: That is, we are honest with ourselves, our colleagues, and our students.

FIGURE 2. CAPS Program Philosophy, Honduras, 1986[1]

4. techniques for teaching speaking, listening, reading, and writing

5. orientation to program materials

6. lesson planning

7. learning strategies

8. microteaching

---

[1] The CAPS program philosophy was developed by 18 Honduran and U.S. teachers from different educational traditions and backgrounds.

Weekly in-service sessions initially focused on discussion of different ways to use the materials, teaching-learning questions (e.g., how to organize cooperative learning), and the solving of classroom problems. After the teachers had become more familiar with the program, materials, and students, the teachers indicated they would like to play a bigger role in professional development. We decided each teacher would be responsible for leading a weekly discussion on a teaching issue or sharing a successful activity. Included among the topics were language experience, a dicto-comp, total physical response activities, questions for critical thinking, effective use of the blackboard, questioning strategies, and wait time.

The end-of-cycle workshops included in-depth instruction on process writing, the integration of language and content, and writing the academic paper—a joint project of the science and English teachers. In addition to these sessions, the English and content teachers organized a series of peer descriptive (nonjudgmental) observations (Fanselow, 1977) wherein they observed one another. These peer observations involved a brief premeeting during which the teacher explained the objectives of the class and how she intended to carry them out, a decision as to whether the observer would simply observe or would actually participate in the class, and a follow-up meeting to describe the observation and discuss how learning was facilitated (the peer observations were possible because the administrative staff taught the class of the observing teacher).

By the end of the second year of the CAPS program, the English teachers had participated in a total of 225 hours of professional development, which were equivalent to 15 continuing education units (CEUs) earned under the auspices of CAL and validated by the Honduran Ministry of Education. In addition, the program provided funding to enable one teacher to attend the annual TESOL convention each year.

Student Acculturation to the Program and Academic Life

Looking at the 1986 program in retrospect, we are a little surprised that some of the academic components we instituted are only now being recognized in the literature. That we established some of the components based on our own experiences of language learning and acquisition is a strong argument for Lortie's (1975) *apprenticeship of observation* and Freeman and Johnson's (1998) premise of teacher knowledge.

Learning Resource Center

The Learning Resource Center was set up not only for academic reinforcement but also to facilitate traits essential to U.S. university academic life: self-discipline, the ability to work independently, and self-monitoring and assessment; all of which lead to personal responsibility and autonomy.

The Center provided a number of activities in four skill areas. Each class of 15 English students spent 1 hour a day at the Center, rotating among the various activities according to their needs and interests, which they had identified in conjunction with their teacher. Center materials were sequenced, and most of them were designed for self-study. The students were required to keep a daily log in which they recorded their activities and reflected on their progress. Two teachers were available in the Center during each period to assist students and to distribute and monitor materials. The Center consisted of five stations:

1. listening and pronunciation
2. extensive reading
3. conversation and other interactive activities
4. video learning
5. computer learning

The students responded well to the idea of choice and programmed learning and proved to be self-reliant, not only in the Center but in their other academic endeavors as well.

The Strengthening of L1 Skills

Following the logic of the transfer of skills from the L1 to the second language (L2) (Cummins, 1979; Lambert & Tucker, 1972), we reasoned it would be advantageous to strengthen the Spanish reading, writing, and grammar skills of our students. Thus, we focused attention on L1 as well as L2 reading.

All students took 2 hours of Spanish, the only content course required during Cycle I. The course was designed to strengthen their reading skills and knowledge of Spanish grammar as well as to introduce or reinforce many of the skills that would be fundamental to their university work. These included learning strategies and critical thinking, the study skills of note- and exam-taking, and the research and discourse skills necessary for a mini-research report. Three of the specific language learning strategies taught were risk-taking (Beebe, 1983), the use of cognates (a bottom-up strategy), and guessing words from context (a top-down strategy).

Figure 3 shows a sample paragraph in English adapted from a newspaper article that most beginning students could understand because of the cognates, but which also required guessing strategies and risk-taking. The students grasped the basic meaning of this paragraph, using its 14 cognates. Working collaboratively, they guessed the meaning of key noncognate vocabulary, taking risks and guessing from context.

In our first evaluation, in answer to a question about what helped them the most in the program, one third of the students commented on the Spanish language component. The following two comments illustrate this response:

> In Spanish I can read things I never read and think about them between the lines.

> Spanish teach me the *detalhes* [details] of getting notes in lecture.

The Honduran-U.S. Culture Component

Although aspects of U.S. culture were interwoven in all of the English courses, Honduran and U.S. culture were specifically addressed in a series of evening lectures. The format of the lecture included the lecture itself, small-group discussion, and recycling and reinforcement the following day through discussion or writing. During the first CAPS program cycle, Honduran history, culture, and beliefs and values were emphasized. Several of the historical lectures concentrated on the Mayan history of Honduras. These lectures were complemented by a weekend excursion to visit the Mayan ruins in Copan, in northern Honduras. In the second cycle, although some presentations on Honduran culture continued, the emphasis shifted to various

Alzheimer's disease is a very <u>serious</u> illness that <u>affects</u> old people. There is a new <u>drug</u> that <u>appears</u> <u>to retard</u> and <u>partially</u> <u>reverse</u> the <u>effects</u> of the disease. The disease is of unknown <u>origin</u> and it <u>gradually</u> <u>erodes</u> brain cells that <u>control</u> thought and <u>memory</u>. It kills 120,000 <u>Americans</u> each year.

FIGURE 3. Cognates in Context

aspects of U.S. culture through another series of lectures. The focus was on intercultural communication, looking at basic beliefs and values. In the third cycle, the concept of intercultural communication was made practical through a series of interviews and home stays with U.S. families in the area. The last part of the culture series focused specifically on adapting to U.S. culture and the academic university environment.

The Honduran culture component was crucial, especially because it established the basis for discussion of other cultures and cultural differences. As the Hondurans became more explicit in talking about their own culture in terms that others would understand, they became more aware of their cultural identity and sense of self. Once their cultural identity was firmly established, they were prepared to learn about U.S. culture without being absorbed by it. The idea of objective respect for one's beliefs and values—whether Honduran, U.S., or other—was introduced early in the program through narrative case studies, role plays, and culture games. By the end of the in-country program, the students were ready to look at cultural differences realistically and with respect.

Socialization: English Language Acquisition Activities

Group socialization activities promoted a team spirit and provided opportunities for the development, strengthening, and exercise of leadership. They also provided the students an opportunity to converse openly and practice their English in an out-of-class environment. Each teacher met informally with his or her class for activities, such as picnics, barbecues, hikes, or parties at least once a month. Various acquisition-rich activities, such as bingo, talent shows, and holiday parties were also scheduled for all students.

Probably the most successful activities were the sports games. We taught the students the rules of U.S. football, basketball, and softball and showed some video footage of the three sports. We also played softball and had a series of softball tournaments. When these students arrived in the United States, they not only understood the rules and registers of the three sports and could talk about them, they could also play at least one of them.

The Integration of Language and Content

As illustrated through the program model, a significant aspect of student acculturation to the CAPS IEP was a gradual transition from Spanish to English academic language and skills development, fostered by an integrated language and content approach to instruction. Math and science courses not only provided students an opportunity to enhance their knowledge in these areas, but also an occasion for them to develop academic language and skills in both Spanish and English. Bilingual teachers could build upon what had been taught through Spanish later in their

English-medium classes, and the English teachers could complement the math and science classes with their attention to academic English. By the third cycle, the English class was focused almost entirely on academic reading and writing, study skills, and strategies (e.g., listening to lectures and taking notes, which had already been introduced in Spanish in the first cycle), and fluency in speaking.

This integration of language and content proved quite successful: Students who had tested at the 7th- or 9th-grade level on the Spanish version of the Comprehensive Test of Basic Skills at the beginning, were testing at the 11th-grade level after the program. (Although this test was not totally appropriate because it was developed for high school students in the United States, it was the only test available for measuring expected content mastery for U.S. contexts.)

◈ PRACTICAL IDEAS

There are a number of practical ideas from the CAPS IEP experience that are relevant to other IEPs.

Management Principles

Incorporate Collaboration and Mutual Respect

The first consideration is management. Whatever happens in an IEP is directly connected to the administrators and their beliefs. The excellence principles discussed in this case study involve collaboration and mutual respect. In our opinion, an IEP director is not a person isolated in an office working with budgets and plans, but someone who is involved with the program, knows the teachers and students, and is so frequently seen in and out of classes that an evaluation is just another instance of an opportunity to discuss or listen to a teacher's decisions, actions, or philosophy in light of the classroom context (Freeman & Johnson, 1998). *In Search of Excellence* (Peters & Waterman, 1982) refers to this characteristic of ubiquitous management as *management by walking around.*

Program Philosophy

Reflect, Discuss, and Suggest Improvement

As a result of the accreditation process, it is not unusual for an IEP to have a written program philosophy. It is a dynamic document that can change as new theories emerge and new teachers become a part of the IEP. Teachers and staff need to reflect on program philosophy, discuss its relevance to the current context, and offer suggestions for modification or addition. If the program is new, discussion can begin with principles and beliefs from daily life because personal and professional lives are so interrelated (Gebhard & Oprandy, 1999). The involvement of everyone in this important process is key and will contribute to unity and program cohesiveness.

Learning Resource Center

Use the Learning Resource Center to Motivate and Facilitate Autonomy

In the CAPS IEP, students spent 1 of 5 daily hours of English in the Learning Resource Center, which had room enough for up to 30 students to work at five different stations. All materials in the Center were available for check-out. Seeing, touching, and reviewing materials was highly motivating, and using materials designed for self-study or programmed learning facilitated student self-discipline and eventual autonomy. In the absence of a Center, a classroom collection or a materials cart, moved from class to class (Henry, 1995), can serve the same function.

Teaching Culture

Contribute to Pride and Identity

Although U.S. culture courses are generally offered at U.S. IEPs, in this program, the point of departure was the students' native culture. This may be difficult in a multi-ethnic class of L2 learners, but a unit that explores the various cultures represented by the class will contribute to ethnic pride and cultural identity.

The Importance of the L1

Strengthen Academic Skills in Both the L1 and L2

Academic language proficiency in the L1 can transfer to the L2. Creating opportunities to strengthen academic skills through the L1 can aid the development of comparable skills in the L2, when a threshold in the L2 is achieved (Cummins, 1979).

Professional Development

Motivate Teacher Learning

A program for professional development (especially one in which teachers can earn credits) will motivate teacher learning, while it also benefits the students and the program. Possible activities include keeping a teaching journal, participating in a series of observations, doing self-observations through video, conducting teacher research, leading informal discussions on what works, and attending conferences and presenting what was learned.

◈ CONCLUSION

This case study has discussed an IEP that was established outside of the United States with U.S. government sponsorship. The distinguishing feature of acculturation of teachers and students to the program and of students, ultimately, to U.S. culture, specifically academic environments developed from our particular context; however it is relevant to any IEP preparing L2 students for U.S. university study. The CAPS IEP design principles were a result of our experience (Johnson, 1996; Lortie, 1975), our particular context (Freeman & Johnson, 1998), and our emerging pedagogy. This included the management principles, the Learning Resource Center, the group-generated program philosophy, and instruction in the L1. The most salient principle of our acculturation and learning pedagogy—the integration of language and content instruction—was a relatively new concept at the time of the CAPS IEP, with much of the work investigating the role of English and the special math and science registers required for successful mathematical problem solving and scientific analysis and reporting (Crandall, 1987; Crandall et al., 1988; Spanos & Crandall, 1990; Spanos et al., 1988). Consequently, we were teachers making sense of our experience, applying that experience to a new context, and considering emerging pedagogy. It was a process of discovery, innovation, making meaning, and then constructing a program. It seems to be that this is the essence of language learning. . . .

◈ CONTRIBUTORS

Patricia Miller has taught in teacher education and directed English language programs in the United States and abroad. She is currently teaching ESL composition at Montgomery College in Maryland, in the United States, and working on her PhD dissertation in second language acquisition at Indiana University of Pennsylvania.

JoAnn (Jodi) Crandall is professor of education at the University of Maryland Baltimore County (UMBC), in the United States, where she directs the Interdisciplinary Doctoral Program in Language, Literacy, and Culture and the MA Program in ESOL/Bilingual Education. Previously, she was vice president of the Center for Applied Linguistics. She is the author of numerous books and articles focusing on curriculum, instruction, and teacher development in content-based instruction and literacy and on language education policy.

CHAPTER 8

Strangers in a Strange Land: An Intensive English Program in an Australian-Korean TEFL Master's Degree Program

Julie Harrington, Marie-Thérèse Jensen, and R. Ruth Rosen

Stranger: n. 1. a person with whom one has, or has hitherto had, no personal acquaintance. 2. an outsider. 3. a visitor or guest. 4. a newcomer in a place or locality.

The Macquarie Dictionary (1991, p. 1728)

◈ INTRODUCTION

As part of the recent internationalization of many educational institutions, collaborative programs have been initiated in universities worldwide. Monash University's internationalization policy, as stated by its Vice Chancellor, aims to "incorporate into all of its activities a way of thinking and acting which is not constrained by national boundaries or traditions and which actively seeks inspiration, understanding and input from outside Australia" (Monash University, 1999). This chapter describes a collaborative teaching English as a foreign language (TEFL) master's degree program developed by Monash University in Melbourne, Australia, and Pukyong National University, in Pusan, South Korea. The "strangers" referred to in the title, therefore, are from Australia and Korea—students and faculty in the two countries who are relative newcomers or outsiders, in relation to one another's education system and culture. A special feature of the program is the pairing of two distinct departments within Monash University, the intensive English program (IEP) and the Faculty of Education, which cooperated to ensure a smoothly integrated program. Of particular interest is the fact that the IEP course is of equal value to other Monash master's-level subjects, not merely a language support class to the main subjects. This case study describes distinguishing features and practical ideas that were successfully implemented in the collaborative degree program.

◈ CONTEXT

Overview of the Program

In 1997 Monash University's Faculty of Education proposed a Master of Education (MEd) degree in TEFL in response to an increasing demand for postgraduate TEFL studies in Australia that could be undertaken by practicing teachers of English from non-English-speaking countries. The agreement for the Monash-Pukyong program was made between the Faculty of Education at Monash and the Office of International Relations at Pukyong National University, in Korea.

The need that forms the basis of the program described in this chapter was for a program that would allow Korean teachers to complete a Monash master's degree in 2 years while continuing to work in their Korean teaching jobs. The final course structure was planned to allow these teacher learners to study for two 5-week intensive periods in Australia during their summer holidays and for more extended periods in their own country during normal university semesters. As one of the principal needs of these teachers was to improve their own oral and written English proficiency, intensive English instruction was considered an essential component in the proposed MEd (TEFL) degree.

The Monash University English Language Centre, a full-fee-paying IEP owned but not funded by the university, delivers intensive English instruction to adult international students. The center had previously developed a close relationship with the Faculty of Education through collaboration in teaching practice, supervision, and observation. It was important to involve both groups in the planning and teaching of the MEd TEFL program because the IEP would form a firm basis for meeting the additional language needs of the Korean teacher learners (i.e., for their postgraduate study and for daily needs living in an English-speaking country).

Prior to the official beginning of the program in Australia in July 1998, two ESL instructors from Monash University spent a semester at Pukyong in 1997, teaching in their undergraduate English program. One teacher was from the Faculty of Education and the other from the English Language Centre. Another role for these lecturers included talking to groups of interested Korean teachers about postgraduate study in Australia and, particularly, at Monash University. They also interviewed each applicant for the program; this gave them an idea of the applicants' level of English and a more personal insight into the educational settings and culture from which these teacher learners had come. During their semester in Korea, the Monash University lecturers offered prospective master's students EFL evening classes to prepare them for the English proficiency test required for entrance into the university's master's degree program.

In addition to sending Australian lecturers to teach in Korea, the plans for the collaborative MEd (TEFL) degree included exchange visits from Korean academics. In 1999 the first Korean visiting academic spent time at Monash University while the students were doing their intensive study there. His presence was valuable because he was able to visit the university classes to get an idea of the content and pedagogical style of the subjects. He also gave a seminar to Monash University faculty relating to the teaching of English in Korea. A number of official and unofficial meetings gave us a better understanding of what the two universities were trying to achieve together: international links in general; the cooperation between the two universities in particular; the desire of the Korean university to train English teachers as researchers; and the motivation of both sides to develop teachers' active, professional use of English in an English-speaking country.

❖ DESCRIPTION

Korean Teacher-Learner Profile

The Korean teacher learners ranged in age from early 20s to late 40s, and about 75% of them were women. They came from a variety of teaching settings, but most worked in government secondary schools and a few in primary and private English language colleges. They were all classroom teachers, although some had positions of responsibility beyond their classroom duties.

Their previous education included a bachelor's degree as a minimum qualification, but a few had completed a master's degree (in Korea), and one had a PhD. All teachers in Korean government schools are required to attend substantial professional development courses; thus, they were quite knowledgeable about the discourse of current language teaching practice. However, most were less confident about incorporating the suggested communicative approaches into their English classes, which typically consist of 45–50 students. This is especially difficult because the Korean examination system largely dictates the teaching program, and reading comprehension still tends to dominate the external examination, despite the fact that a series of educational reforms is underway. It is therefore not possible for these Korean teachers to use a typical Western concept of communicative language teaching without making considerable adjustments to their own system of EFL education.

Subject Timetable and Course Content

The MEd (TEFL) degree consists of five subjects and a research project. The degree program commences at Monash University in Year 1 with the first two subjects studied in an IEP mode during 5 weeks in the July–August intensive period. Table 1 shows the program structure. The course descriptions that follow illustrate linkages among subjects and the importance of the IEP components of the degree.

TABLE 1. MED (TEFL) COURSE STRUCTURE

Year	Timetable	Monash University Courses		Pukyong University Courses
1	July–August (5 weeks)	IEP's Advanced English for Professional Practice in TEFL	Theory and Practice of TESOL	
	September–December			The International Context of TEFL
2	March–June			Curriculum Design in TEFL
	July–August (5 weeks)	Research Design in TEFL	Minor Research Project* IEP Writing Workshops	

*The minor thesis is due in June of the following year.

IEP Advanced English for Professional Practice in TEFL

This course focuses on the development of academic writing and professional communication. Students also practice accessing information and using multimedia for their own language learning. They are exposed to IEP classroom observation and teaching practice, along with a wide range of materials for teaching. They also observe language classes in Melbourne schools at the primary (elementary) and secondary school levels. This class links language learning and professional practice. The challenge is to provide a range of materials and activities that develops the understanding of already highly proficient language teachers as well as their classroom pedagogy.

The IEP class is conducted at Monash University over a 5-week period for 16 hours per week (80 class hours). Because the teaching takes place in the Monash English Language Centre, the Korean teacher learners can attend classes for observation quite conveniently. The general objectives are to

- develop confidence and skill in spoken English
- upgrade knowledge of communicative language teaching methodology
- introduce Australian English language teaching practices
- introduce a variety of computer-assisted language learning (CALL) programs and possibilities
- develop a variety of speaking and listening activities easily utilized in the classroom
- encourage critical reflection on materials and texts presented
- visit Australian schools

This IEP course is structured around two modules (Language in the Classroom and Writing and Speaking as Professionals) and four learning units:

1. promoting and managing interaction in the classroom
2. using written language in the classroom
3. developing and presenting writing for professional purposes
4. presenting work orally

Theory and Practice of TESOL

This course examines the concept of language proficiency and surveys second and foreign language education over the past 40 years. Sessions focus on aspects of foreign language teaching, such as the development of language skills, vocabulary, grammar, integration of language and content, materials development, lesson planning, and CALL.[1]

After completing the first two intensive courses at Monash University (120 class hours), the Korean teacher learners return to their teaching jobs and to Pukyong National University to complete the third and fourth subjects, outlined below, over two semesters in evening classes. These classes are taught entirely in English by

---

[1] Experiences in teaching these first two IEP courses form the discussion of the Distinguishing Features and Practical Ideas sections of this chapter.

Korean lecturers who have an excellent command of the language and so serve as models of successful learners of English.

The International Context of TEFL

In this 40-hour course taught at Pukyong University, students look at recent trends in the use of English internationally. They explore in detail linguistic variations in spoken English, including phonetics and phonology, and analyze educational policy in relation to the learning of English in Korea.

Curriculum Design in TEFL

This course explores models of curriculum and syllabus design, approaches to needs analysis, policy, and assessment tasks and systems. Students develop a curriculum plan they can support with current theory and research on language learning and teaching. They draw on their knowledge as teachers of EFL and on their own experience as EFL learners in discussions of curriculum design.

Students return to Monash University in July–August of Year 2 to complete the fifth subject, Research Design in TEFL, and to begin the minor research project, which is to be completed by June of the following year, under distance supervision from Monash University.

Research Design in TEFL

In this course, students are provided with guidelines and detailed input about conducting and writing up research in TEFL. They are also given practice in developing a full research proposal, including a rationale, aims, literature review, and research design. Students look at different approaches to the investigation of teacher and student interaction, classroom discourse, learner styles and strategies, and classroom practices.

The Research Project

In this final component of the MEd (TEFL) program, commenced during the second IEP phase at Monash, the teacher learners write a minor research paper of 10,000 words that explores actual teaching and learning contexts in Korea. This research project is supervised by Monash staff from the Faculty of Education. Before students and supervisors are matched up, potential supervisors describe their own research interests and invite questions and discussion from the learners. Guidelines are provided for conducting and writing up research in TEFL during a series of intensive academic writing workshops. The learners then return to Korea and complete the research project in distance mode. With the help of their supervisors, they obtain ethics approval and develop a detailed proposal prior to embarking on the research. Supervisors assist learners with the practical issues involved in conducting the research and advise them on the process of handling data.

◈ DISTINGUISHING FEATURES

Subject Design

A distinguishing feature of the IEP component of the program was that the subject design was predicated on a number of specific teaching and learning assumptions different from the regular teaching focus of the Monash IEP, which prepares students for academic study in Australia. Because the Korean teachers were working concurrently on intensive English studies and on their MEd TEFL degrees, they needed practical experience in English learning environments upon which they could reflect through journals and class discussions in light of theory and practice, using English as the medium for communication.

The actual process of learning and using English for reflection, discussion, argument, and lesson preparation was empowering for the Korean teacher learners. During the 5-week IEP, the group shared materials and produced a collected booklet of workable lesson plans, which they each received as a tangible resource at the end of the course. The group and the instructors created an excellent dynamic of collegiality throughout the 5 weeks. This continued into the following year, bringing with it a substantial support network for the program and future teaching. This first cohort saw themselves as part of a vanguard in the changing of the status quo of English language learning and teaching in Korea. The process of participating in an advanced-level IEP in an English-speaking country was an important intellectual, social, and emotional experience.

Use of Thinking Logs

An innovative aspect of the collaboration within the first two courses of the master's program was the use of *thinking logs* in which participants reflected on the content of the Theory and Practice of TESOL course, but were assessed within the Advanced English for Professional Practice in TEFL course. Nixon (1996) documented the insights arising from journals of Vietnamese teachers studying in Australian TESOL programs. The Vietnamese teachers were asked to focus on adjustment issues with the aim of assisting Australian teachers to better understand the cross-cultural concerns arising in international courses. Many other researchers have noted that journals are a valuable process in documenting cultural and learning experiences and relating them to familiar home professional and cultural knowledge (e.g., Mayher, Lester, & Pradl, 1983; Porter, Goldstein, Leatherman, & Conrad, 1990). Thinking logs in our program are a type of journal that focuses on developing understandings (e.g., for this course, about the theory and practice of TESOL) through readings and classroom discussion. The scope of the journal in Nixon's study was more general than that of the thinking logs and included students' personal reactions to their change of country and lifestyle (see Appendix A).

Reflecting on Class Observations and Readings

The Korean teacher learners were not asked to keep journals of their new experiences, cultural adjustment, and language difficulties while studying in Australia, yet many of the formal and informal discussions covered the differences and adjustments they needed to make during the 5-week period. Like the journal keepers in Nixon's study who, in line with the suggestion of Mayher, Lester, & Pradl (1983), focused on "reactions to class experiences, making connections with previous experience and . . . techniques" (Nixon, 1996, p. 29), the Korean teacher learners found the thinking logs an excellent vehicle to clarify and reflect upon their understanding of particular approaches to language learning. They were asked to relate an approach or methodology to their class observations as well as to speculate how it might work within their own teaching and learning environments. They were also obliged to reflect on readings and discussions that were taking place in the Theory and Practice of TESOL class, comment critically, and link theory to their own experiences, both in Korea and during their observations at the Language Centre at Monash University. They were expected to raise questions and reveal their thinking processes in a clear and logical manner as well as correctly cite and reference authors, as preparation for the papers and research aspects of the master's program.

Reflecting on Communicative Language Teaching

The thinking logs were also used to address one key question for the participants: To what degree is it possible and desirable to adapt modern communicative teaching approaches to the Korean school teaching situation?

Before studying in Australia, the Korean teacher learners had had very different amounts of exposure to the idea of a communicative or meaning-based approach to the teaching of English, including the idea of using spoken language in the classroom. They also varied in their opportunities to apply a communicative approach in their work. Teachers at private language institutes had smaller classes and a more flexible syllabus than did the teachers at secondary schools.

By the time they wrote their second thinking log, the Korean teachers had viewed a video (Institute of Languages, 1994) that showed a teacher presenting a grammatical structure (e.g., *should have/shouldn't have*) in a function that was typical of that structure (e.g., criticism of past actions). The approach is known as Presentation, Practice, Production (PPP).[2] In the PPP video, the context of the presentation was meaningful for the learners. The context was set by the teacher, who asked about what the learners had or had not done to prepare for their recent class test. A controlled practice stage followed the presentation, which included much drilling of pronunciation features. Finally, in the production stage, students engaged in a number of small-group interactions based on real life-like scenarios. The PPP video gave the Korean teachers the opportunity to see a lesson that set out to teach linguistic forms in a meaningful way. This was a practical introduction to the communicative approach.

The thinking log of one Korean female secondary school teacher summarized differences between this meaning-based approach (the PPP lesson) and a traditional grammar-based approach she had experienced as a school learner:

> Let me check the difference between PPP model class and my previous English class. First there was no presentation stage compared with the class in the video. My teachers just referred directly to grammatical terms and explained how to write or change the sentences (e.g. change active voice sentences into passive). The explanation was not related to my interest or lives. And then we practiced a lot of sentences that were in the grammar book. At that time the examples in the grammar book were not relevant to me. So I had many difficulties understanding grammatical terms and catching the

---

[2] Presentation, practice, and production is an approach to lesson planning that focuses on the teaching of language structures in use. It has been made popular internationally by training courses for the Certificate of Teaching English as a Foreign Language to Adults (Cert. TEFLA), which is run by the Royal Society of Arts, and the University of Cambridge Local Examination System, UCLES.

facts in my text. I didn't have the chance to practice speaking. Just I wrote down on the notebook. The production stage is very important to practice speaking. It must include my experience and my life. Why? Some day I will talk about my life. It was almost ignored. I think it made me a disabled speaker. I had few opportunities to listen to my or others' speech.

This student reflects on two features of the communicative approach as described by Larsen-Freeman (1986): One is that new language presented in class must have meaning for the learners. The second is that learners need opportunities for using the spoken language.

The term *communicative* was used in the title of three students' thinking logs written in the fourth week of the course. Two other thinking logs discussed group work or interaction. Five other logs contained *speaking* or *spoken language* in the title, two more talked about listening. In these logs, students came to grips with the principles identified in class as well as features specific to the communicative approach, such as negotiation of meaning, information gaps, choice, feedback, and tolerance of errors. Above all, students wrestled with the practical problem of introducing speaking activities to large groups of students (40+) sitting in fixed rows in an EFL class in their country.

A number of students reported on the activities they had observed at the English Language Centre as part of their Advanced English for Professional Practice in TEFL class:

> [T]he class I observed largely consisted of three activities. First, the students solved two group tasks after reading instructions and writing the answers individually, and second they did role-play according to their own chosen characters in the story. It seemed the students had enough time to speak each other out of these activities. More importantly, students seemed to feel comfortable when they talked each other, since the teacher endured most of their errors, as she intended, just to encourage them to speak freely and fluently.

Most of the students acknowledged the value of teaching speaking skills but had not tried it out. In contrast, one student reported on his own use of group work in a secondary school in Korea. He explored the topic of group work at some depth in his third log, written toward the end of 4 weeks of intensive study. He noted the importance of group work in the IEP class, in class readings, and in the practice of the English Language Centre teachers in Australia. He linked this to requirements of the Korean Ministry of Education, writing that they "are asking us to make more opportunities to interact with students in groups, pairs and individually considering students' level." He went on to say:

> In Korea many secondary school teachers are reluctant to give students an opportunity to do group work. The reasons are similar to those mentioned by Penny Ur. She said, "Teachers fear they may lose control, that there may be too much noise, that their students may over-use their mother tongue, do the task badly or not at all" (Ur, 1996, p. 232). I also share these same such concerns as she said when I tried group work in my class for the first time. When the concern became reality, I would have given up that kind of lesson, (but I thought) that a silent class could not be the evidence they were really studying well. I had students select one leader of each group. I drilled the

leaders until they got accustomed to group working. One week later they began leading the other members skillfully and even began competing with other groups in order to get the higher group score. These days they are enjoying group work very much. And also their English scores have been improved much more than the students of other classes who don't work in groups.

The process of understanding what the communicative approach includes, and considering how it might apply to the Korean EFL teaching situation, continued for these teachers on their return to their country. The first cohort of teachers were, at the time of writing, engaged in collecting data for their research projects. Some of the teachers were undertaking action research projects that aimed to develop their students' use of English in meaningful contexts.

Emphasis on Academic Writing

In the IEP, the results and outcomes in terms of grades were high: The thinking logs were all in the upper ranges; the lesson plans/miniteaching and the two tests were less uniformly well-executed, and there were two low grades, but most results were very high overall. We were, therefore, unprepared for the subsequent issue that arose when the Korean teacher learners returned to Korea. Once they began sending in their final papers for the Theory and Practice of TESOL course, it became clear that, in fact, they lacked understanding of the structure of traditional Western academic writing and had an insufficient grasp of referencing conventions.

We began to rethink the problem and realized that we had based our planning for the English course on certain presumptions: that the teacher learners were sufficiently proficient in English; that they had all achieved around 6.0 across all skills in the International English Language Testing Service examination; and that they were all interested in self-development, hence their desire to complete the MEd (TEFL) degree. Moreover, once the group arrived in Australia, we made other assumptions: first, that their fluent control of the vocabulary and discourse of spoken academic language was equally applicable to their academic writing; second, that the students would imitate the genre of the academic readings and transfer it to their own writing; and third, that the semiformal academic journal writing (thinking logs) would give them sufficient practice to cope with future formal essay writing.

Our assumptions about the teacher learners' communicative fluency had blinded us to the need for a specific teaching focus on the genre of Western academic writing. Consequently, the students had far greater difficulty than we had anticipated in writing good academic papers. The false assumption made with the first cohort of Korean teacher learners was redressed by means of several focused essay writing workshops when they returned to Australia for the second intensive period. For the second cohort, the IEP was adjusted to include more emphasis on academic writing.

The overall benefits of the IEP course, Advanced English for Professional Practice in TEFL, outweighed the specific problem. Student evaluations indicated that all aspects of the course were considered useful and enjoyable. Students were asked to comment on the Day One orientation sessions, specific class work, thinking logs, library tours, school visits, microteaching sessions, computer classes, excursions and social activities, classroom observations, and final examinations. They were also asked questions in line with the course objectives, such as about their confidence in using English, expressing an opinion, speaking in public, writing more fluently, understanding the academic demands of the university, the social network, the course teachers, and, generally, their view of the probability of success in their MEd (TEFL) program after completing the IEP component.

◈ PRACTICAL IDEAS

For colleges and universities wishing to set up a similar program, we offer suggestions that our experience has shown contribute to success.

Carefully Choose Participants for the Program

Teacher learners' level of spoken English needs to be fairly high, and individual weaknesses in syntax should not interfere with the ability to express complex ideas. Diversity of age, experience, and professional background among the cohort is most useful for raising issues arising from theory.

Begin With a Strong Orientation Program

The introduction of the learning environment, teachers, and support staff, along with a description of the broader context of location and extracurricular activities, is important on the first day. An outline of the units of learning and a clarification of expectations and assessment criteria should also be discussed.

Integrate the Units Within the IEP Course to Intersperse Theory and Practice

Issues for teaching methodology and practice, particularly in light of the program's focus on the communicative approach to English language teaching and learning, need to be included. Tutorials need to focus on theoretical readings and discussions, along with regular class observations and discussions. Microteaching to peers can be an added dimension of teaching practice in English. CALL workshops should be included for skills and knowledge of integrating programs, along with material development and school visits for diversity.

Create Classroom Observation Record Sheets

Class observation protocols should focus on lesson timing, teacher presentations, class management, teaching aids, and student production. (For classroom activities and observer's own ideas and comments, see Appendix B.)

Use Thinking Logs For Self-Awareness as a Learner and Teacher

As noted earlier, the use of thinking logs for critical reflection can be an extremely valuable learning tool for teacher learners. Preparing to write encourages learners to read with attention. It also heightens their awareness of issues raised in class discussions and gives more focus to their language lesson observations. The process of writing the logs also allows the learners to develop fluency in writing. In addition, their ability to think critically and analytically is sharpened by the need to express their thoughts in writing. Finally, writing the thinking logs is a way of pushing the learners to incorporate new understandings into their own practice.

Ensure That the Genre of Western Academic Writing Is Specifically Taught and Internalized

Fluency in speaking and in informal writing can be misleading; competency in academic writing is vital for all papers and the final thesis in this program. As the instructions for writing thinking logs indicate (see Appendix A), learners may write the logs as they think them through. Thus, the language they use may be informal. On the other hand, academic writing of essays or longer papers in the western tradition requires both formal language and formal structure.

Create Clear Assessment Points

In the IEP course Advanced English for Professional Practice, assessment was based on the requirements below:

- thinking logs
- a lesson plan, which indicated intended level or age of learners, objectives of the lesson, language and learning theories being used, learners' and teacher's roles, and materials needed
- a minilesson teaching demonstration (15–20 minutes), which was analyzed, discussed, and evaluated by the group as well as by the instructors
- a two-part examination, which included a reading comprehension passage and a short essay

Create Clear Criteria to Earn More Than a Passing Grade

The students in our program were assured of a passing grade if they completed and submitted all the work requirements. To receive higher than a passing grade, student work should demonstrate critical analysis rather than pure description, there should be reflection on theory and practice, and there should be correct referencing.

◈ CONCLUSION

In summary, the inclusion of an intensive, advanced English component in this master's degree program was essential. The Korean teacher learners realized that the chance to improve their own English proficiency greatly enhanced their ability to teach their EFL students more effectively.

Since the beginning of this collaboration in 1998, there has been steady development of understanding among all the individuals involved in the program in Korea and Australia. We are no longer strangers, but we still have much to learn from one another. After 2 years of working in the program, with our first cohort of Korean teacher learners approaching the end of their studies, we on the Australian end have paused here to describe the offerings of the program and to reflect broadly on its progress to date. We look forward to further collaborative research with our Korean colleagues for continued success of the program. We hope that this account may assist other teams of IEP specialists and TESOL teacher educators to clarify their own curriculum aims in such joint ventures.

◈ CONTRIBUTORS

Julie Harrington is a lecturer in the Faculty of Education, at Monash University, in Melbourne, Australia. In 1997, she spent a semester teaching in the English Department of Pukyong National University, in South Korea. She teaches the Research Design in TEFL course in the MEd (TEFL) Program at Monash.

Marie-Thérèse Jensen is a lecturer in the Faculty of Education, at Monash University, where she teaches the Theory and Practice of TESOL course in the MEd (TEFL) Program. She has taught IEPs to adult immigrants in Australia and to international students in Europe and Japan.

Ruth Rosen is director at the Monash University English Language Centre. She is currently working on her doctorate at Monash University, in the field of international education and policy. She has a particular interest in teacher development.

◈ APPENDIX A

Instructions for Writing Thinking Logs[3]

Requirements

The purpose of this task is for you to respond as often as possible, in writing, to the readings and discussions in the course, in light of your own experience and as a record of your developing understanding of the issues you find most interesting.

Keep all journal entries in a single folder, which is to be handed in on the following three dates:

You should write a minimum of three journal entries (i.e., at least one entry for each submission date). Write the date of each entry at the top of the page. Only one entry will be assessed at each submission date. If you make more than one entry for a given date of submission, choose which entry is to be assessed and indicate this by clearly marking "Assessment" before the date.

Your log should:

- focus on topics that you choose yourself (arising from course material and/or discussion)
- refer specifically and comment critically on one or more readings on the topic
- make links between theory/research and your own experience
- reveal your own thinking about the topic
- include your own questions
- be around 500 words in length

Your log may:

- be expressed entirely in continuous prose

---

[3] The instructions for writing thinking logs were adapted from the original outline provided by Rosemary Viete.

- include diagrams/charts/tables of your own devising to help you sort out your own and others' ideas

- be handwritten or wordprocessed (double-spaced in either case)

Please Note

- The language you use may be informal; you may write it as you think it through.

- A summary of the reading is not required. Making a summary can be useful background work but does not replace the reflective activity of writing a thinking log.

Thinking Log Assessment Sheet

Name of student:

Submission date:

Topic focus:

1. refers directly to readings distributed in class
2. refers to other relevant readings
3. comments critically on readings
4. makes links between theory/research and own experience
5. reveals own thinking on the topic
6. includes own questions
7. keeps to recommended number of words
8. is clearly presented
9. organizes ideas well
10. uses English accurately and appropriately

Comments

Sample Thinking Log

Log Entry For Week 2 on Grammar Teaching

As grammar holds an important position in teaching English in Korea, I have been interested in teaching grammar efficiently since I became an English teacher. But traditional grammar translation method could not help me create fresh and new ideas. My teaching became a little stale. Fortunately, last week I had an opportunity to observe a grammar class here at the language center which inspired me. I saw some techniques that I could use to teach grammar more effectively and interestingly. It was an inductive approach toward grammar teaching in context and had a variety of practices that combined with communicative functions.

The class I observed had the teacher teaching a class the simple present tense. She presented her students with more than five sentences that use the simple present tense verbs and asked them to find out any of the common rules among the sentences. Her students seemed to enjoy the process of founding them out and could approach its grammar naturally and inductively. In area of inductive or deductive methods, Penny Ur (1996) tells us; Teachers have to decide whether to elicit the rule from the learners on the basis of inductive method, or give it themselves, and invite them to produce examples (deductive). In that respect, I think that the teacher chose the correct method, inductive method, because the level of students was intermediate and they could perceive and define the rule of the present tense themselves quickly and easily.

Another interesting method she used was that she presented the situations and when to use them as habitual time, truth/laws of nature, concurrent time, frequency, future time and past tenses. This way may prove to be a meaningful way that they could learn how and when to use the expressions.

Also she taught the simple present tense in context. She presented a passage with some blanks. Students filled in the blanks with proper verbs. They could familiarize them with the structures in context, giving practice both in forms and communicative meanings. They could also learn in what situations the grammar should be used.

Grammar separated from context is meaningless in learning English. For instance, if anyone learned a simple present tense separated from context (e.g., *I go to church every Sunday*.), the learner could not understand that the sentence can also refer to habit. Then he or she may gain a scrappy knowledge of the simple present tense of *go*. And also if we explained grammar deductively as in this example: In the sentence *He goes to church on Sundays*., adding *es* behind *go* is because the subject *he* is the third person singular pronoun, and you can use simple present tense in order to refer to habit, it would be too abstract to apply the rule to another sentence easily. Actually, the rule could confuse the students. This could also create an uninteresting class and the student could lose interest. The problem is that that kind of explanation can take place in Korean classes.

In Korean Secondary Schools, it is true that many teachers approach teaching grammar only deductively. There seems to be some reasons for this. First, the English textbooks consist of many grammatical terms and contents to elicit their grammar rules. But the bigger problem is that teachers are made to complete the required material in the books due to the examination mandated by the board of education. This then causes the teachers to go along at a quick pace and cannot afford to think of inductive approaches to teach the grammar, as trying to do this would require more time than the teachers are given. Secondly, there are too many students in a class to allow enough time to practice what they learned in a communicative way.

Despite these problems, I found a good way to solve these complex problems. Combining Penny Ur's definition of grammar and the observed lessons, I can say that grammar teaching must be combined with communicative functions, which means teaching grammar in context.

◈ APPENDIX B
Checklist

Monash University English Language Centre
MEd TEFL Classroom Observation Checklist

Date:	
Class Level:	
Teacher:	
Number of Students:	
Teaching Aids Used:	

As you observe the class in action, make notes or write comments about the following issues. These will be the basis of your own class discussions and thinking logs. There is also space at the end for you to add any other comments about the observation. Think about skills being taught, strategies used, and the metalanguage for transitions between activities as well as theories and methods.

Aim of the Lesson:

What is the aim of the lesson?

How does the teacher make this clear?

Do the students understand the aim?

Teacher-Centered or Student-Centered Class?

How can you tell?

Teacher awareness of differing student needs:

Interaction Within the Class:

Teacher-student:

Student-student:

How Does the Teacher Motivate the Students?

Lesson Organization: Presentation of New Material; Summary of Previous Work, Development, and Feedback

Is the class well-organized?

Classroom Management:

Reluctant students:

"Problem" students:

Different levels:

Different nationalities:

Questions:

Many or few?

Who asked the questions?

How were they dealt with?

Error Correction:

Individual:

Class:

Dealing With Vocabulary:

Introducing new items:

Dealing with student questions about vocabulary:

Teaching Materials:

Visually interesting?	yes	no
Appropriate?	yes	no
Professional?	yes	no

Additional Comments:

PART 3

Breaking
New Ground

CHAPTER 9

Credit Courses? It's Time!

Mary Brooks

◈ INTRODUCTION

Intensive English programs (IEPs) are coming of age in the United States. Many IEPs are now highly regarded by the universities and the communities to which they belong. It is not unusual for programs to be 20 years into the maturation process. Our communities are realizing that we are here to stay.

When IEPs are recognized as viable and even indispensable to their universities, the students in turn receive the respect that they deserve and are further motivated to excel (Martino, 1992). Students exiting from English language programs demonstrate that they have gained a high level of language proficiency, developed skills in academic learning, practiced higher level thinking skills, and engaged in interactions with professors and peers in culturally appropriate ways. They are not only bilingual but bicultural with respect to thinking and learning strategies. This ability to use a second language to pursue an academic degree demonstrates the rigor of a student's language preparation within the IEP. Van Meter (1990) states that "the acquisition of a new language requires as much or more effort than is required of typical college level courses" (p. 4). In order to be successful, students must understand the cultural and rhetorical context of the target language that in some cases can be quite different from their own first language and culture. Van Meter also points out that the skills required in ESL courses are as complex as those required in foreign language courses and are different from those required for remediation in first language skills.

Because credit is the university's way of sanctioning course work, IEP courses should be granted university credit in recognition of the high level of language proficiency attained by their students. Although some have argued that university standards are lowered by offering credit for ESL classes, many today would say that offering credit does not devalue the university but encourages diversity and honors students' achievements from a multicultural perspective (Martino, 1992).

At the English Language Institute (ELI), at Eastern Washington University (EWU), it was decided that ELI students should be given credit for advanced-level ESL courses. In 1997, we applied for credit status for four existing ELI courses, and the proposal was accepted by the university's Undergraduate Affairs Council. The following is an account of the rationale and process through which we worked in order to gain credit status for English language course work.

◈ CONTEXT

The ELI was established at EWU in 1978. For more than 20 years, the ELI has experienced growth, curriculum development, recognition of its faculty, accreditation by the Commission on English Language Program Accreditation, membership in the Consortium of University and College Intensive English Language Programs and in the American Association of Intensive English Programs, and a strengthened relationship with the university. Seventy-five to eighty-five percent of the ELI students matriculate into university studies at EWU.

The ELI participates in the university in many ways. We are part of the Modern Languages and Literatures Department. We work directly with the College of Education and Human Development, the College of Business and Public Administration, and the School of Music in promoting joint programs. The English Department collaborates with us in the ELI exit/English Department entry testing. We hire international peer advisors, full-time EWU students who help in our orientation process, which is a way to provide U.S. students the opportunity to interact and network with international students. We also cooperate with Housing and Dining Services, helping them understand the needs of international students. In short, we are working in a context of success and positive interaction with our university.

The ELI comprises five levels of language instruction. Level 5 reflects advanced language acquisition equal to, if not greater than, the requirements of other foreign languages at the 300 and 400 levels. Courses at this advanced level of the ELI each contain cultural aspects of language, rhetoric, critical thinking skills, and the analysis and summary of library materials collected for research. Successful completion of Level 5 courses is required for recommendation into university studies. The courses include Writing for Academic Purposes, Reading for Academic Purposes, University Seminar, and Research Paper. Writing for Academic Purposes is cross-listed in the English Department for international students who enroll directly into the university without taking the ELI course sequence. (See Appendix A for the overall ELI/English department course sequence and course descriptions for Levels 4 and 5).

Students can now receive undergraduate credit for ELI Level 5 courses. They can decide whether to take these courses for credit, using an ELIC prefix (C = credit). Some do not need the credit because they are transferring credit from their home universities, or because they are on a study abroad program for a short time and will return to their home countries. These students register with an ELIN (N = noncredit) prefix.

◈ DESCRIPTION

For the past 15 years, a recommendation from the ELI and acceptable transcripts have been sufficient for students to matriculate into EWU. The expertise of the ELI has been recognized as a basis for this matriculation. Two years ago, we decided that it was time in the life of this program to add the credit component to advanced course work. Once that had been accomplished, students at Level 5 of the ELI would be treated no differently from other students fulfilling modern language requirements at the university.

ELI faculty decided that the total number of credits for the four courses at Level 5 would be 18. This number was partially arrived at by adding up the credits of required course work in a foreign language for native speakers of English, which was

15, and adding three more credits that could be counted as an elective course in university graduation requirements. Not all courses in the ELI would be granted credit; otherwise, the total number of credits at graduation would be too heavily weighted in one area (i.e., English language). Politically speaking, we thought we stood a better chance of success if we asked the Undergraduate Affairs Council for 18 credits for ELI course work than if we asked for more. Proposing 36 credits for ELI Level 4 and Level 5 course work probably had little chance of passing through the university committees. Most likely, we would have had to defend ourselves against those who argue that ESL classes are remedial. Proposing only Level 5 classes offered an easier case for showing an advanced level of language skills. The four advanced level courses chosen for the credit proposal were all existing courses in the ELI (i.e., Level 5 courses).

What follows is a description of the steps we took in preparing the credit proposal, steering it through university committees, and finding support within the university community.

Preparing the Credit Proposal

The following description of a Level 5 course, Writing for Academic Purposes, contains the rationale, course objectives, methodology, and evaluation included in the proposals we wrote for credit status. Although the requirements for other universities may differ, these sample descriptions might be used to frame the writing required by other IEPs seeking credit for their courses. The proposal writing genre is retained in order to help readers understand the process and compile their own proposals. (See Appendix B for course proposals for Reading for Academic Purposes, University Seminar, and Research Paper.)

Rationale for the Course

ENGL 111, Writing for Academic Purposes, is already a credit-bearing course in the English department for second language students (5 credits). Students coming directly from their home countries to EWU with a minimum TOEFL score of 525 (paper-based test)/193–197 (computer-based test) take a writing placement exam. English 111 is a placement option for these students. Students from the ELI can also be placed in ENGL 111 as a result of the ELI exit/English department entry exam. The current Level 5 Advanced Writing course and ENGL 111 are very similar. Level 5 Advanced Writing should become ELIC/N 111 in order to avoid duplication at this level.

There will be three populations of students in this class. One group will consist of students who have been accepted into the university with a TOEFL score of 525 (paper-based test)/193–197 (computer-based test). Another group will be ELI students who have reached advanced proficiency level in writing and have been accepted into the university. In order to clarify the course sequence, ENGL 111 is cross-listed with ELIC/N 111 for these two groups. For a third group of ELI students who will not be matriculating into EWU, the course number is ELIN 111.

In this way, the ELI and the English Department will work together to retain ELI students at EWU because the ELI students will be able to matriculate into the university sooner. (At present some students go to community colleges to complete their English requirements.) Further, ENGL 111 enrollments will stabilize, facilitating enrollment management. The preparation for further course work in the English Department (ENGL 112, 101, and 201) can be addressed more systematically, expediently, and collaboratively.

The two departments, the ELI and the English Department, have used the same exit requirements for the past 8 years for Level 5 Advanced Writing. This same exit assessment is conducted at the end of each quarter to determine who is ready for ENGL 112 or, in some cases, ENGL 101 (Freshman Composition). Some students need to stay in ELIC (N)/ENGL 111 for another quarter until they are ready to move into ENGL 112.

This course is only for students who speak English as their second language. The enrollment is restricted to placement or advising from the EWU international student advisor, the ELI student advisor, or the ESL advisor in the English department.

Course Objectives

The purpose of this class is to help students improve written fluency through a variety of writing styles: journaling, free writing, and academic essay writing. They also improve their writing style through practicing sentence combining and reduction of clauses. A further objective is to expand their productive grammar skills and their range of vocabulary. Students continue to work on critical thinking skills and also receive instruction on strategies to avoid plagiarism.

The goal of the course is to prepare second language students to function in university-level courses and to be able to demonstrate knowledge of English language syntax, phonology, morphology, semantics, and pragmatics.

Methodology

In order to increase communicative proficiency in writing, a variety of methodologies is used. The primary method is a communicative approach that allows students to interact in English among themselves and with the instructor on a daily basis in a variety of contexts. Students often act as peer editors for each other. Peers also help each one generate ideas. This class is student centered, with the teacher serving as guide and facilitator.

Evaluation

Students must demonstrate their competence in all previous levels in the ELI or be placed into this class on the basis of a writing sample at entry. The testing in this class is cross-graded by cooperating teachers. Standards for this course are part of the total program standards for the ELI in collaboration with the English Department.

Evaluation is divided into several areas, reflecting the nature of the course:

Essays	20%
Grammar	10%

In-Class Tests	10%
Midterm	20%
Final Test	30%
Participation, Attendance	10%

A grade of 3.0 (on a scale of 4.0) is required to pass this course, reflecting the necessary level of language proficiency required to meet further demands in the sequence of courses and the university.

❖ DISTINGUISHING FEATURES

Steering the Proposal Through Committees

Throughout the process of gaining credit for ELI classes, a number of institutional requirements had to be anticipated and met. First, in order to recommend the advanced-level courses for credit status, we had to write an initial justification. This document had to be submitted as an undergraduate new program or program revision to the Committee on Program and Course Change and to Undergraduate Affairs Council. Second, we worked with the English department to show that there was no redundancy in the ELI and English department courses and that the courses followed the English department requirements. Third, we worked with the Department of Modern Languages and Literatures to show that our courses were on a level consistent with upper division foreign language courses. Fourth, because it was necessary to show that the ESL courses were beyond remedial, showing congruency to upper level foreign language courses was useful.

After all the committee work was completed and signatures were in place, these course changes were written into the EWU catalogue. The proposal writing, the discussion with the departments involved, and the gathering of signatures was largely the task of the ELI director. At all times, we had the support of the dean of the College of Arts and Letters.

Finding Support Within the University

The process of seeking credit for our courses has served as a forum for disseminating information about the IEP within the university community. Going to departments and requesting cooperation was a positive step in the promotion of the IEP. Finding supporters and informing departmental advisors about the IEP in turn helped advisors encourage international students already in the university to take our courses for further language support. Furthermore, the credit-bearing status of Level 5 classes has become a recruiting advantage, not only for the English Language Institute, but for other cooperating departments as well. In addition, it has encouraged international students to remain on our campus to matriculate into other university classes, rather than going to area colleges in order to circumvent EWU requirements.

Overall, this process has shown us ways to promote international student education and gain university support at the departmental, committee, and administrative levels.

◈ PRACTICAL IDEAS

A number of factors must be taken into account in preparing a successful proposal for credit classes.

Describe Your Program

Assume little knowledge about the program on the part of your committee readers. Many instructors in the university community know little about special programs. Start from the beginning. Summarize the progression of the program showing its development as intrinsic to the university. How long has it been in existence? Carefully describe the levels and show how the IEP enables students to be ready for university/college studies. Do you belong to national organizations as a program? Are you accredited by the Commission on English Language Program Accreditation? In this way, you can show how your IEP is similar to existing departments.

Describe Your Relationship to the University or College

Is the IEP involved in cooperative programs in the university? What kind of departmental support do you enjoy? Does your faculty take part in committee work in the university/college? Also, explain the reporting system in your college. You need to show that you work under similar if not the same rules as other departments do.

Include Your Mission Statement

Explain this statement. Describe how your IEP fits the institutional mission statement with respect to its commitment to internationalism and diversity. This is an important step in the rationale building. It helps committee members understand the position of the IEP as a channel for students to enter the university or college. For some programs, this contribution of internationalism and diversity might be significant.

Offer Statistics

Document the number of university-bound students. Support your case for credit classes with statistics whenever you can. Showing numbers of students quickly translates into economic contributions that your IEP makes to the university.

Consider Foreign Language Requirements
When Making Credit Requests

It is difficult to decide how many credits to request as you write your proposal. To help you decide this number, consider the foreign language requirement at your institution. If 15 quarter credits account for the foreign language requirement, request this number. You can add some course work for elective credits. Find a way to make your proposal fit into the system already in place. Do not ask for too much.

If possible, choose a number with the prefix code that is in sequence with other classes for nonnative speakers in the university/college. In our case, we designated ENGL 112, a writing class for nonnative speakers in the English Department, as a coordinate number. In this way, the IEP numbering system was congruent with existing numbers in the university and could be recognized.

Show How IEP Courses Reflect College-Level Requirements

Most of the arguments against credit ESL classes come from the perception of ESL as remediation (Hafernik & Burgamy, 1985). It is helpful to point out how the IEP credit classes are congruent to the advanced levels of foreign language classes offered to native speakers of English. Hafernik and Burgamy (1985) have stated, "ESL classes are not remedial in that they do not repeat material previously presented and not mastered. Rather they contain an academic component as well as developmental component" (p. 5). Show the academic and developmental components of the classes.

Find Support

Garner support from modern languages faculty. They teach the courses most equivalent to IEP course work. Compare modern language courses to IEP courses at the advanced to superior range on the ACTFL Guidelines (Shrum & Glisan, 1994). Show equivalency to modern languages at the upper levels of French, German, and Spanish.

Show Full-Time Equivalency

Show full-time equivalency (FTE) value in the possible numbers of students added to departmental count. If you are not an independent department, your FTEs can be counted by your host department. This is important because many universities' funding models are based on student FTE (i.e., the number of students enrolled in credit courses). It is crucial to show economic value wherever you can.

Use Cooperative Strategies

Propose teaching assistantships as a cooperative means. In some universities the teaching assistants can only work with credit classes to fulfill their assistantship requirements. The credit bearing status of the IEP classes can sometimes allow the possibility of this cooperation.

◈ CONCLUSION

At EWU, we have found eight positive results in the credit-seeking process.

1. There is greater support for the ELI from the university and our host department, Modern Languages and Literatures, because we are making a direct contribution to the full-time equivalent student count, which affects university and departmental funding.

2. There is greater support for ELI students because of the additional choice of taking classes for credit or noncredit.

3. Going through the committee work to get credit status has given the ELI more recognition from other university faculty.

4. The ELI student advisor works with students at the intermediate levels to help them prepare for university entrance. Because students who take credit ELI classes must already have acceptance into the university, this advising becomes more real because of the credit status of the classes.

5. The registrar's office pays more attention to the ELI because our students register alongside other regular students at the university.

6. Credit classes have provided a pedagogically appropriate placement for nonnative speaker citizens and permanent residents who still need English language instruction. Many of these students have similar linguistic needs to international students that can be addressed in these courses. Because these courses provide credit, these students can also continue to receive financial aid.

7. Offering credit classes has helped stem the attrition rate to area community colleges because there is more motivation to stay at EWU.

8. It has become easier for us to ask for classroom space because the ELI classes bear the same credit weight as other university courses.

9. Despite its clear advantages, credit status can sometimes create adverse results for the IEP and its students. However, it is possible to minimize these potentially negative results. Some majors do not accept elective credits, so it is crucial to counsel students carefully and note the catalogue requirements to make sure it is in the students' best interest to take the IEP classes for credit. In addition, the cost of credit courses is sometimes higher than the IEP fees. Show the students how time can be saved by taking the classes for credit. Another potentially complex issue is the division of tuition money between the university and the self-supporting IEP. A percentage of money has to go back to the IEP from the university when IEP students enroll for credit. Work needs to be done at the provost level to make sure this money goes back to the IEP. Show how the IEP budget suffers if nothing is returned because the IEP would be paying for teacher salaries but would not be receiving tuition fees.

In 1997, the English Language Institute at Eastern Washington University completed the process of gaining credit status for four classes at the advanced level. We are happy with the status this change has offered. We hope that the university will see second language students as a population with distinct academic promise rather than as a population with remedial problems (Van Meter, 1990). The process of creating the credit classes has given us more reasons to go to other university departments and seek cooperation. As a result, there are fewer barriers to the professional acceptance of our ELI. Overall, the process and results have been positive. It was the right time in the life of this IEP to take one more step into the university community.

◈ CONTRIBUTOR

Mary Brooks is the director of the English Language Institute (ELI) at Eastern Washington University, in the United States, where she has been employed for the past 12 years. She teachers in the ESL Certificate Program for Teachers as well as in the ELI. She has had extensive experience teaching abroad in Korea, the People's Republic of China, and Zambia.

◈ APPENDIX A

English Language Institute
Course Sequence

The italicized courses are taught by the English department. All other courses are taught by the ELI.

Course Number	Course Title	Contact Hours/Week
Level 1-Novice		
ELIN 061	Listening/Conversation Level 1	7
ELIN 071	Reading/Writing/Grammar Level 1	10
Level 2-High Novice		
ELIN 062	Listening/Conversation Level 2	7
ELIN 072	Reading/Writing/Grammar Level 2	10
Level 3-Intermediate Low		
ELIN 063	Listening/Conversation Level 3	7
ELIN 073	Reading/Writing/Grammar Level 3	11
Level 4-Intermediate High		
ELIN 064	Notetaking and Discussion Level 4	7
ELIN 074	Reading/Writing/Grammar Level 4	11
ELIN 095	Computer Skills	1
ELIN 096	Advanced Computer Skills	1
ELIN 087	Advanced Grammar Workshop	2
ELIN 088	Pronunciation Workshop	2
ELIN 098	Electives	
Level 5-Advanced		
ELIN/ELIC/ENGL 111	*Writing for Academic Purposes (5 credits)*	5
*ELIN/ELIC 113	Reading for Academic Purposes (5 credits)	5
*ELIN/ELIC 114	University Seminar (5 credits)	5
*ELIN/ELIC 116	Research Paper (3 credits)	3
ENGL 112	*Writing: English for International Students*	

(* = courses that are usually taken concurrently to ELIC 111/ENGL 111. N indicates noncredit. C indicates credit. Students have the option of taking these classes as N or C.)

Course Descriptions: Levels 4 and 5

ELIN 064   *Note-taking and Discussion Level 4*

Exposure to wide range of materials. Practice in note-taking, organizing, summarizing and using information to speak and write. Presentation skills, interviewing, and problem solving are also emphasized.

ELIN 074   *Reading/Writing/Grammar Level 4*

Exposure to a range of text types, both ESL and authentic. Continued use of reading strategies to enhance reading proficiency. Higher level thinking skills are encouraged and reflected in the expository writing required at this level. Academic essays, using patterns of rhetoric, writing a thesis statement, journaling, free writing, and grammatical accuracy are the emphasis of the course. Process writing is practiced.

ELIN 095   *Computer Skills*

The focus is basic computer keyboard competency. Students practice basic keyboarding skills, writing and editing texts using a word processor (MS Word), using email, and researching on the World Wide Web.

ELIN 096   *Advanced Computer Skills*

Extended practice in basic computer skills and use of programs. Students learn a variety of ways to search for and evaluate information on the World Wide Web, use and organize email, and revise texts using MS Word.

ELIN/ELIC/ENGL 111   *Writing for Academic Purposes Level 5*

An integrated skills course to develop writing and grammar fluency in a variety of writing modalities through reading, writing, and discussion to prepare students for the multifaceted demands of academic writing.

ELIN/ELIC 113   *Reading for Academic Purposes Level 5*

An integrated skills course that uses essay and narrative at a university level to develop advanced skills in reading, writing, critical thinking, and discussion.

ELIN/ELIC 114   *University Seminar Level 5*

An integrated second language skills course focused on listening and note-taking that prepares students to discuss issues in seminar. Emphasis is given to analyzing, synthesizing, and evaluating university level content from lectures and general university requirements class observation.

ELIN/ELIC 116   *Research Paper Level 5*

An advanced course designed to familiarize students with the process of writing a research paper, synthesis of multiple sources, critical thinking, avoiding plagiarism, and use of library and internet resources.

◈ APPENDIX B: COURSE DESCRIPTIONS

ELIC 113—Reading for Academic Purposes (5 Credits)

Rationale

The American Council on the Teaching of Foreign Language (ACTFL) Guidelines describe proficiency levels across language. Reading for Academic Purposes in English as a second or foreign language is congruent with the 300 and 400 levels of German, French and Spanish. This course is also analogous to English 111 and English 112 as courses for international students that are credit bearing.

Reading for Academic Purposes reflects a high level of language proficiency. The ACTFL Guidelines describes the advanced level of reading proficiency in this way: The student is able to follow essential points of written discourse in areas of special interest of knowledge; understand parts of texts that are conceptually abstract and linguistically complex, and texts that treat unfamiliar topics and situations, as well as some texts that involve aspects of target-language culture; and comprehend the facts to make appropriate inferences (Shrum & Glisan, 1994). The student also has an emerging awareness of the aesthetic properties of language and of its literary styles that permit comprehension of a wider variety of texts, including literary text types.

This course is only intended for students who speak English as their second language. The enrollment would be restricted to placement and advising from the international student advisor or the ELI student advisor.

Successful completion of this course is already required at the English Language Institute for matriculation into university course work. Students who enter EWU with a TOEFL score could take this course as a way to enhance their skills in the area of reading. It would also be a way to offer a bridge course for special programs in the university.

Reading and writing are often taught in conjunction; writing is taught as a response to reading. However, the skills of writing and reading are quite different and need separate time in the sequence of course work, thus requiring the need for an independent reading course at this level.

Reading tasks at this level are large in scope, tapping higher level thinking skills, requiring little time for direct recall and obvious points of comprehension. The material is rich in meaning with well-selected themes that lend themselves to reflection in discussion and writing. There is exposure to a wide range of text types, including journal articles, authentic narrative (not abridged), and sources from the Internet. There is also an emphasis on critical discussion both orally and in writing as follow up to reading. This course should be credit bearing, reflecting the proficiency level required.

Course Objectives

The purpose of the course is to help students: continue to develop critical thinking skills, use writing and discussion as a part of the reflective thinking process in reading, describe the author's perspective, recognize literary devices and patterns of organization, make inferences, and increase the enjoyment of reading a wide variety of text types and literature.

Methodology

In order to increase communicative proficiency in reading, a variety of methodologies is used. The primary method is a communicative approach that allows students to interact in English among themselves and with the instructor on a daily basis in a variety of contexts. In this way, the reading class is student centered, that is, it takes place in a classroom where the teacher is a facilitator and can best help prepare students to be independent readers.

Evaluation

Students must demonstrate their competence at all previous levels before they are allowed to take this course. Consistent standards are applied across all levels and subjects. All testing is collaborative, that is, tests are cross-graded by cooperating teachers. Standards for this reading course are part of the total program set of standards as approved by the Commission on English Language Program Accreditation.

Evaluation is divided into several areas, reflecting the nature of the course:

Reading Tests	30%
Vocabulary Work	10%

Projects	10%
Homework	10%
Final Test	30%
Class attendance and participation	10%

A grade of 3.0 (on a 4.0 scale) is required to pass this course, reflecting the necessary level of language proficiency required to meet further demands in the sequence of courses and in the university.

ELIC 114—University Seminar (5 Credits)

Rationale

University Seminar is the highest level course available in the English Language Institute, an English for Academic Purposes program. It provides practice at the advanced level in all language skills. The focus of the course is note-taking in academic lectures; these notes become the source of seminar discussion.

The skill of conversation is an integral part of University Seminar. Discussion and presentation skills, affect and paralinguistic features are all part of the work of this course, reflecting an advanced measure of language proficiency. Summary writing is also a requirement of the course, enabling students to synthesize lecture material.

The lecture content presents a range of social, political, and economic issues. In order to consider the issues raised, the students gather data, not only from lectures given by EWU professors, but also from reading essay material, and using the Internet. Issues at this level are problems with complex, debatable solutions; there is a need for description, analysis, synthesis, and evaluation of ideas.

This course is required of all students in the English Language Institute as a mark of reaching a level high enough to be recommended for further studies in the university. The skill expectation in a second language is advanced.

A student already in the university may be advised to take this class when more skill practice is needed in the areas of listening to lectures, note-taking, and discussion.

Course Objectives

This course will help the student listen to and comprehend lectures in content areas of instruction offered at EWU. The student will take notes, using symbols and abbreviations and later demonstrate recall of significant detail, grasp of main ideas, and organization by using these notes to paraphrase, summarize, ask, and answer questions, and take content tests. The student will take part in discussion based on the lectures.

Methodology

Lectures, usually offered by EWU instructors, are given on a regular basis in order for the students to practice note-taking skills. These notes are used as students form groups to discuss, analyze, and summarize the key ideas. These discussions generate writing tasks. The teacher is a guide through these processes; as soon as the students understand the task at hand, they are expected to carry out the requirements, both individually and as a group.

Evaluation

Evaluation in the ELI is program wide. The testing is collaborative. For University Seminar, discussion groups are part of the testing process. Two teachers evaluate the students in these test sessions. Written work is also cross-graded by two teachers. Evaluation is divided into several areas, reflecting the nature of the course:

Listening and Note-taking		Discussion	
In class lectures	30%	Group Presentations	30%
Unit tests	20%	Individual Speeches	10%
News Journal, Homework	10%	Midterm	20%
Final	30%	Final	30%
Participation, Attendance	10%	Participation, Attendance	10%

A grade of 3.0 (on a 4.0 scale) is required to pass this course, reflecting an advanced level of language proficiency.

ELIC 116—Research Paper (3 Credits)

Rationale

Research Paper is an integrated skills course. The goal of this course is to further develop advanced language skills through the production of an extended piece of writing. This is essential to working within the U.S. university system. Through assimilation and synthesis of data from a variety of sources, the student learns the skill of research, in this case, reviewing the literature.

Planning, selecting data, organizing, citing references, and writing an 8- to 10-page paper in a second language is an advanced task. The student uses writing as a process of analysis, uses higher level thinking skills to read and describe the literature, and uses the library and the Internet as resources. The issue of plagiarism is also a critical piece to the course. Class time is used to differentiate between paraphrasing, summarizing, quoting, and copying. The level of competency required in this course is advanced and should be recognized with credit.

Course Objectives

The student will be able to produce a paper of 8–10 pages by writing a provisional thesis and outline, using library and Internet skills to locate information, finding materials and deciding what is useful, writing reference cards, taking notes, synthesizing material by paraphrasing, summarizing, quoting, and drawing conclusions. The student will use these steps to refine the thesis and outline, write a rough draft, and edit and revise the draft with teacher assistance and peer advice. Finally, the student will continue using the computer to write a final draft using appropriate referencing and bibliographic form. The final goal of this class is a presentation of the thesis and main points of support in order to stimulate discussion among the student peer groups.

Methodology

The teacher is a guide and writing mentor throughout this class. The majority of the work is accomplished in small peer groups and by individual writers. Problems common to the class are used as points of class presentation, for example, grammar and editing issues. The teacher also models quoting, paraphrasing, and summarizing, showing the differences between these skills and plagiarism. The students in the class act as peer editors for each other.

Evaluation

Evaluation is divided into four areas showing that promptness and responsibility, process, product, and presentation are all important factors in the building of a research paper. The Research Paper grade should reflect readiness to write another paper rather than the production of a perfect paper. The minimum requirement of 3.0 (on a 4.0 scale) is required to pass the course and to show advanced proficiency. The Research Paper grade will come from these four areas:

Attendance	15%
Process	40%
Final Paper	30%
Presentation	15%

CHAPTER 10

Reaching Out to the Hard to Reach: Helping Learning Disabled Students

Robin L. Schwarz

◈ INTRODUCTION

This chapter describes a program of the English Language Institute (ELI) at American University (AU) in Washington, D.C., that aims to help students who are considered at risk because of a learning disability or other learning challenges. The program grew out of my desire to find out if students were failing their intensive English program (IEP) classes because of learning disabilities and, if so, to help them get support similar to that provided to native-English-speaking students with learning disabilities so they could successfully continue toward a degree.

◈ CONTEXT

The ELI is a medium-sized IEP of 400–500 students, the primary purpose of which is to prepare international students to enter the university. Because of the provision that international students can begin their degree classes before fully finishing their non-degree English requirement, the program has a mixture of nondegree and degree undergraduate students as well as graduate students and a few IEP-only students. English classes are offered at six levels, with the first four being intensive at 20 hours of class per week; the fifth a support level, with 10 hours per week; and the sixth, a credit class (freshman composition for international students). The curriculum is skills based, which permits students to be in different levels of reading, writing, listening/speaking, and grammar. Students are tested separately in the four skills for placement. Undergraduates are required to complete the IEP courses that placement and subsequent follow-up diagnostic testing indicate they need. Graduate students are instructed by their departments and advisors on how much of the recommended IEP course work they must take.

The student body of ELI is drawn from more than 80 countries, with students from Asia and the Arabian Gulf states making up the largest part. The majority of students have studied English for many years, typically in middle and high school, and some in postsecondary settings, resulting in a low demand for ELI's beginning-level classes. Often no Level 1 classes are run, and the sections of the Level 2 skills may be quite small. Approximately 20 teachers, most full-time, make up the teaching faculty.

◈ DESCRIPTION

A major source of frustration for teachers, administrators, and students in an IEP is student failure despite everyone's best efforts. Typically, failing students work hard and attend regularly, yet they do not make progress. Failure could well mean the end to an eagerly anticipated academic career or at least another semester in the IEP.

The usual explanations for second language learning difficulties—anxiety, poor language learning habits, lack of opportunity to practice, lack of motivation—do not readily apply to foreign students admitted to study in a U.S. university. Undoubtedly, some of the students do not practice their English sufficiently, preferring to stay within a group of friends of the same language and culture, but most use English in the dormitories and in classes as well as in off-campus activities. Motivation comes in the form of personal goals for a degree, but just as often in the form of pressure from scholarship sponsors or parents who might cut off funding if no progress is evident. Although poor language learning habits definitely could be a factor in explaining lack of progress, many students quickly understand that they will have to work hard to survive and pick up such skills readily. Realizing that these reasons did not explain all student failures, in 1989, I decided to find out if some of these students could be struggling with a learning disability.

In the United States, learning disabilities are understood as neurologically based difficulties with taking in, processing, or producing information. These difficulties can affect reading, writing, speaking, listening, thinking, organizing, or doing mathematical operations. Learning disabilities are lifelong and do not diminish over time. A learning disabled person may have average or above average intelligence, but has difficulty learning in standard ways (Gerber, 1998).

In the late 1980s and early 1990s, native-English-speaking students diagnosed with learning disabilities in U.S. universities were beginning to be able to obtain legally mandated accommodations, waivers, or course substitutions if they had difficulty in meeting their foreign language requirement. It seemed logical that foreign students struggling with their English requirement should have access to the same considerations. However, the situation for them was quite different. The notion that the ESL students in college or university settings could have a learning disability was practically unheard of, and in the rare instance where the possibility was considered, the existing services for native-English-speaking students were essentially denied to the ESL students. Service providers often felt that they could not communicate well with the students in interviews where testing or accommodations and other important ideas would be discussed. They also felt that cultural issues would be a problem in diagnosis and service delivery. Although these qualms were undoubtedly justified to a certain extent, there nonetheless existed the clear possibility that there were ESL students with learning disabilities who were suffering unnecessarily in unsuitable classroom situations because their needs were not properly recognized.

As a field, ESL became aware of the impact of learning disabilities on the second language learners in the elementary and high school populations starting in the late 1970s, largely because bilingual specialists had objected as the special education ranks in schools began to swell with referrals of limited-English-proficient students. Models were developed to help teachers and schools determine which students might have a learning disability and which were merely showing normal language learning problems (Ortiz, Robertson-Courtney & Wilkinson, 1990). However, for the college ESL student, the idea was basically unheard of until the 1990s, and still today, few English programs and teachers are aware of learning disabilities or trained to assist such students.

In the 1980s, Ganschow and Sparks (1995) began research on native-English-speaking college students who were failing in their foreign language classes. Their findings supported Dinklage (1998), who said that learning disabled students were extremely likely to have trouble with second language learning. More intriguingly, researchers found that, sometimes, even if a student was competent in his or her first language, problems could arise in second language acquisition (Sparks, Ganschow, & Javorsky, 1992). According to Ganschow and Sparks (1995), these problems seemed to be caused by intrinsic processing deficits that could be subtle in the first language, but significant when a second language was involved. This fact, combined with the finding that approximately 5–10% of the general population has a learning disability significant enough to interfere with normal learning (NICHCY, 2001) made it highly probable that many of the failing students at ELI had learning disabilities. The challenge was to devise a relatively easy way to spot them and then to establish protocols for helping them.

Thus, prompted by the frustration experienced by teachers, administrators, and students themselves with the unexplained failures and by the lack of services for and knowledge about learning disabled ESL students, I designed a two-part program to address these problems at our IEP. One part was a procedure for screening and providing support to individual students; the other was a specific IEP writing course designed to aid in the assessment and to meet the needs of at-risk learners, most of whom were identified during the placement process.

This two-part design did not happen immediately. At first, when the suggestion to find out if the failing students actually had learning disabilities was proposed, students who were at the brink of dismissal or whose failure record was alarming were simply sent to me for evaluation. Because I had a background in the field of learning disabilities as well as ESL, I looked for certain performance patterns typical of learning disabilities and interviewed students to find out if there was a past history of problems. Students who met those two criteria were referred to outside specialists for further diagnosis. The students' classroom teachers were then helped to understand the problem and given suggestions for interventions that might help the students to function better in class (e.g., giving the student extra time where needed, giving instructions and homework assignments in oral and written form, or not grading spelling in compositions and on certain kinds of tests).

Once teachers were made aware of identifiable symptoms of a learning disability, they began to refer more students. The program was enthusiastically supported by the academic counselor and the university's acting provost, who approved release time so that I could serve the increasing number of students being referred. Finally, nearly 5 years after the informal process began, The Learning Skills Program (LSP) came into being and the position of learning skills advisor (LSA) was created formally, and I accepted it.

◈ DISTINGUISHING FEATURES

As noted earlier, the LSP offered two components:

1. screening and support services for individual students already in ELI
2. a class for special instruction designed to meet the specific needs of incoming students identified as at risk for failure, possibly because of learning disabilities.

Student Screening and Support Services

Once formalized, the procedure for referral of a student already in ELI was relatively simple. Teachers gave me information, which I checked against the student's records, then had an interview, perhaps did some informal screening, and made recommendations for further action (e.g., referral to a specialized optometrist, recommendation for tutoring, interventions in ELI classes, communication with the student's teachers from other disciplines). I then communicated the outcome or pending actions to the student, teacher, and director so that everyone was aware that the student was being helped. As many as 20 students a semester were referred for evaluation.

However, this sort of intervention was not terribly successful. For one thing, once students were referred, it took time for many of them to understand the notion of learning disabilities and the process of finding out about their possible problems and appropriate support. In some cultures and countries, the notion of a learning disability being a cause for failure in school is unfamiliar (Ijiri & Rooney, 1995; Rooney & Schwarz, 1999). The academic advisor and I felt, therefore, that students who showed signs of learning disabilities could be given more thorough support in learning and help in understanding their learning situation in a class setting. Even if a formal diagnosis did not happen, we reasoned, these students would have a better chance of succeeding. Furthermore, a lack of effective study habits can contribute significantly to ESL students' failure (Schwarz & Terrill, 2000), and the advisor and I had noticed that these students did not successfully access the resources available to them on campus (e.g., the library and its multiple resources, the campus writing center, and their academic, non-ELI advisors). Direct instruction early on in study skills and other survival skills seemed another way to reduce the students' problems.

Special Instruction

Besides the desire to help students understand their problems and to teach them study and academic survival skills, the knowledge that in other schools, students with learning disabilities were successfully being taught foreign languages in classes especially designed for them motivated our program to try something similar for the ESL students. Downey (1992), at the University of Colorado at Boulder, found that students with learning disabilities had a better chance of succeeding in a foreign language when teachers used principles of teaching known to be helpful to learning disabled students in general and addressed the students' phonological deficits through a structured multisensory presentation of the sound system of the target language.

With these factors in mind, one writing class per semester was designated for students who were at risk of failing. We chose a writing class because the students flagged were more at risk for failure in writing than in other skills in the ELI program.

The special writing class, as it came to be known, consistently enrolled 12–18 students. This was not an ideal size because personal attention and individualized instruction were goals. Nonetheless, that number of students—roughly 10% of the incoming students each term—was flagged as at risk according to the screening process used in the program. The process grew out of the findings of Sparks, Ganschow, and Javorsky (1992), who found that phonological processing problems are prevalent in poor language learners, with poor spelling and grammar as a corresponding result. Poor visual memory, which also figures in poor spelling, is another symptom of a learning disability.

Because many ELI students had studied English for a long time, it seemed reasonable to expect (indeed years of writing samples indicated) that most would have learned fairly adequate spelling and grammar in English. Therefore, when a student's writing sample on the ELI placement test had an unusually high number of spelling and grammar errors, I was given the composition. If, in contrast to the many errors, the writer had written a long essay and had fairly strong vocabulary and thoughts, then its author was flagged as at risk.

Sometimes samples could have many errors but also have hardly anything written on them. At that level of production, it is difficult to know if the problem is still a lack of English study or a learning disability. Those students were usually placed in the lowest levels for a semester until it could be determined if they were making progress. Although many at-risk students had unusually poor handwriting, a problem many learning disabled persons have (Gerber, 1998), that in itself was not a sufficient indicator because many of the ELI students are writers of Arabic or other languages that do not employ the Roman alphabet and could possibly be learning new orthography in a new direction.

An exception to that generalization are the Japanese students, who are drilled vigorously in orthography, and whose handwriting in English is almost always excellent. When a Japanese student's composition showed poor handwriting, his or her work was immediately looked at more closely. It was not unusual in this informal screening process to find that students flagged as at risk also had highly discrepant placements within the ELI system. They often placed out of listening and speaking classes, had varied placements in reading, and placed low in grammar and writing. This pattern conformed to what Ganschow and Sparks (1995) found in their study of poor language learners: Many may have adequate phonological skills to converse in a language but are not able to master the grammar and writing because of weak semantic and syntactic skills.

Students placed in the special writing class were told on the first day that the purpose of the class was to help them improve their writing and learn effective academic skills. ELI has several days of diagnostic testing in class to confirm the findings of the placement test. A student in the special class who produced better writing during diagnostics than in the placement test was transferred to another section.

Another motivation for having the special class was to incorporate some of the teaching techniques that Downey (1992) found appropriate for learning disabled foreign language learners (Schwarz & Terrill, 2000), so the special class was conducted somewhat differently from other writing classes in the IEP. First, despite being college level, the class was highly structured for the students. Notebooks were required, and students had to carefully sort handouts and other papers into appropriate sections so that they could readily find them. Included in this notebook was a weekly grid on which assignments were copied as given. Students then had a reliable record and could not protest that they had not heard, remembered, or found an assignment. Although students balked at first, many reported later that they continued to use that notebook structure for themselves in other classes.

Similarly, information such as instructions for assignments, key vocabulary, or explanations of lessons was presented in oral and written form and in the same way at all times. Students whose listening or reading skills were weak learned that they could depend on having essential information in a format they could predict.

As mentioned earlier, being able to emphasize academic survival skills was a primary purpose of the class. Phone numbers of other members of the class as well as contact information for the teacher were provided so that students could never offer the excuse of not knowing what happened or what was assigned in class—a frequent cause of students' falling behind in academic classes.

Similarly, attendance was strictly monitored . A passing grade depended heavily on regular attendance. Besides ensuring that they were present to learn, this requirement was intended to help students get over old habits of avoidance. They typically skipped class when a paper was due or a test was scheduled and then would attempt to make up things. Once they understood their grade depended on their being in the class, however, they began to find ways to be there. There was a similar requirement for homework, as handing it in was as important a part of their grade as quizzes or attendance. The at-risk students were slow to understand this aspect of U.S. classes, which was often quite different from their experience in their cultures, and they needed some extra incentive to absorb its importance.

Three other features of the class that differed from regular classes were

1. the pace of presentation
2. the amount of information presented
3. the amount of reteaching and review that took place

These features were included because learning disabled students typically do not process information quickly or efficiently and because memory overload is a problem (Downey, 1992; Gerber, 1998). The syllabus was pared down to the basics for the special class. Unlike the regular writing classes, in which four or five rhetorical patterns of writing might be taught, patterns in the special class were limited to a critical two or three, which students practiced repeatedly. Outlining was stressed as well to help impose logic and order on writing.

All of the material presented was reviewed in as many ways and guises as possible. Such activities as finding topic sentences and supporting ideas in reading passages, rewriting poor topic sentences, or quickly structuring the support for an outline were used to revisit the skill of writing topic sentences in many ways. Grammar and spelling were not ignored, but neither were they stressed unduly because remediation was not the purpose of the class. Students were taught some methods to improve their spelling, which was also one of the aims of the phonological instruction described below. In addition, they frequently rewrote assignments to practice correcting some of their spelling or grammar mistakes, but the papers were evaluated primarily on how well students handled a particular writing element, such as topic sentences or transitions between paragraphs.

This focus relieved students of a great deal of worry and frustration; nonetheless, we also stressed to them that they had to work hard to hand in corrected papers for other professors—whether by using a spell checker on their computers, dictionaries, or just by paying attention to words they used in exercises they were completing or in texts they were writing about.

Finally, because Ganschow and Sparks (1995) have shown a clear causal connection between poor phonological skills and poor language learning, phonological instruction was included in this special class. Some students needed it more than others, but, generally, students were retaught the vowel sounds until they could discriminate, read, and spell them with near mastery. Then they were taught rules of syllabication based on long and short vowel patterns. This phonological instruction was aimed at strengthening not only reading and spelling, but listening comprehension and pronunciation, according to the findings of Ganschow and Sparks (1995). From the reports of students themselves and of their teachers in other skills classes in ELI, such instruction appeared to be successful.

The special class started at the third level of writing at ELI, but the students were offered the option of remaining together and moving to the next level with their teacher. This provided a familiarity of setting and predictability of routine and expectations that learning disabled students tend to need. Indeed, as far as their schedules permitted, the ELI students chose to stay in the special class through the highest level.

Outcomes of the Program

As might be expected, the outcomes of this intervention varied enormously. The primary goal of the program was to accurately identify those students who might have a learning disability so that they could be helped more specifically by referral for official diagnosis and support from the learning skills office on campus. The second goal was to decrease the number of failures among at-risk students by giving them a more personalized learning environment. More students were identified, but not as many as the academic counselor and I had hoped. For one thing, many students were unwilling or unable to understand the diagnosis of their learning situation. No matter how carefully it was explained to them, some chose to ignore the help offered until dismissal from the program was imminent. Other students failed courses or left for other reasons.

A few had such severe problems that they could not be successful in the AU setting because the IEP could only offer help in the writing class and because the AU services for learning disabled students did not include daily tutoring and guidance. Some of these students were referred to other settings where that support was available, but more often than not, the most severely affected failed and were dismissed. Many of the dismissed students moved on to other English programs, where the whole process would start all over again. Others decided that the effort of studying in English was just too much and chose to go home.

Nevertheless, teachers as well as the director of the IEP, the academic counselor, and I felt that although the intervention was not a panacea for all at-risk students, it did help more students to stay in the IEP and to succeed at the university than before it was offered. Furthermore, it is a practice not commonly found in English programs, and the students knew it and appreciated our efforts. Many reported that no one before had explained why they were having such a hard time in school when they knew they were as intelligent as their classmates. Many also said they definitely would not have been able to stay at AU without an LSP.

◈ PRACTICAL IDEAS

The following five suggestions make it easier to create the services discussed in this chapter .

Obtain Administration and Faculty Support

A successful network of intervention resources for the students in the IEP requires the support of the administration and the teaching faculty. I would not have continued as the LSP at AU if the director and other university authorities had not endorsed the idea. Even the Learning Services Office at AU, though committed to helping students with various problems, needed to be convinced before it would receive and work with international students diagnosed with a learning disability if they had low English skills. Similarly, if the teachers had not been involved in the program through education and cooperation, fewer students would have benefited from it. Thus, groundwork is necessary for success.

Identify Students in Need

To determine if a student who is having a language learning problem might have a learning disability, teachers can ask the following five questions.

1.   Has the student's problem persisted over time? Students who have a learning disability make little progress in areas where they are weak. Students may report or teachers observe that similar problems exist in the first language, or that they have studied English for a long time without significant progress.

2.   Has the problem resisted regular instruction? The first response of teachers to a student who cannot read well or makes lots of spelling errors is to think that the student must not have been taught English phonics or rules for spelling, when in fact, the student may have been taught phonics in many different courses or been tutored intensively in spelling. Such information indicates that the student does not learn easily.

3.   Does the student have irregular performance in the ESL class? It is often hard to decide if a student has a learning disability because the student does some assignments well or answers questions in class brilliantly but then does the next few assignments poorly or cannot understand what is happening in class. Or in certain activities the student is competent, whereas in others, which to the teacher may seem simpler, the student has difficulty. This makes teachers think the student is lazy or willfully not keeping up, but in fact, this irregularity is the most common charac-teristic of learning disabled students.

4.   Does the student have clear strengths and weaknesses outside the ESL classroom? Students in the LSP were often gifted artists, talented with

computers, or strong in science or economics. The inconsistencies noted above are seen on a larger scale here. Student may not reveal their strengths in the ESL class. Learning disabled language learners often show this pattern by being fluent in English but significantly weaker in writing or reading.

5. Does the problem interfere with academic or life goals? Everyone has strengths and weaknesses, but when weaknesses impede school success or obstruct obtaining a necessary license or a better job, then they are handicapping weaknesses. For ELI students, not being able to complete the English requirement often means not getting a degree, which in turn may be critical for a particular job in their country. It was to help students avoid these unnecessary defeats that the LSP was started (Schwarz & Terrill, 2000).

If the behaviors described in these five questions are coupled with a student's concern and frustration at not making progress, then looking for a learning disability would be appropriate. Therefore, when a student has a problem that persists over time and resists regular teaching and the student's best efforts, and if the student exhibits clear patterns of strengths and weaknesses both in and out of the classroom, then a learning disability could well be the cause (Schwarz & Terrill, 2000).

Obtain Student Information

The next part of identification is obtaining information on the student. Comments or evaluations from teachers could confirm the persistence and nature of problems such as poor spelling or a poor homework record, or excellent effort but no progress. Transcripts and records from other schools may show hints at problems, such as if the student has failed in other foreign language courses, or did only adequate work in studies of his or her own language. The typical discrepancy in strengths and weaknesses could be hinted at in above average grades in subjects with less emphasis on reading and writing, and poor grades in classes requiring writing, speaking, or reading. However caution should be used in interpreting transcripts because grading scales are different, and concepts of poor work vary across countries and cultures.

Other causes of poor performance need to be ruled out, but typically these affect not just specific areas of learning, but the whole spectrum. For international students in postsecondary settings, issues such as difficulties with housing, scholarships or money, difficult roommates or family problems could affect academic performance, but in a far more universal way than a learning disability will.

Visual difficulties, too, could cause many problems that look much like dyslexia, a reading disability, or like dysgraphia, a writing disability (Vuko, 1997). In the usual eye exams, problems affecting distance sight are identified, but these exams do not identify problems with accuracy of vision. These problems are caused by the musculature in the eyes not working correctly. Some specialized optometrists treat these visual problems with visual therapy; others prefer to prescribe prisms that compensate for the distortions or poor musculature. Rarely, the problem may result from untreatable problems in the eye. With glasses with prisms, students can immediately see and read much better, indicating that these are not learning disabilities, which by definition cannot be cured. Since the problems resulting from poor vision are much like those caused by learning disabilities, eliminating that possibility is essential early on. Students in the special writing class at ELI and all referred students were first screened for such visual problems.

Assess the Educational Situation

Once other issues, including visual difficulties, have been eliminated and a student has been tentatively identified as likely having a learning disability, the educational situation must be assessed so that a decision about further diagnosis can be made. As mentioned, it was not unusual for a student who was having difficulty with English language courses to do well in content courses. This fact, combined with the reluctance of students to go for a diagnosis and the high cost of it, may lead to a decision to teach students better academic survival and self-help skills, and to provide support to teachers so they will know how to work with these students more successfully.

On the other hand, if a student's problems are significant, a legal diagnosis of learning disabilities will be required, and he or she will need formal accommodations, such as legally mandated extra time, exemption from penalties on spelling and grammar problems, oral testing and/or special help on papers.

The diagnostician ideally should be bi- or multilingual and should be given as much history of the student's problems in English classes or other classes as possible, as well as a clear idea of the challenges the student faces at the school where she or he studies. With this knowledge, in the report, the diagnostician should include recommendations to the school and to teachers for the support and intervention that would be most helpful for the student's success. These could include those already mentioned above, as well as permission to tape classes and have a note-taker or reader for tests and important assignments. These are the type of accommodations requiring legal documentation of a learning disability that American students with learning disabilities are entitled to and benefit from, and that international students rarely receive.

Consider Instructional Issues

Finally, consider instructional issues. Besides the support and interventions recommended by the diagnostician, the techniques used in the special class at ELI can be beneficial to learning disabled students. These include having more structure, both in out of the classroom, a slowed pace of learning, required material pared down to essentials, visual and auditory presentation of everything, opportunities for multisensory review, reteaching, and an accepting atmosphere. Two other considerations that often are of great benefit to learning disabled students are unlimited time on any kind of test and alternative testing.

Other interventions recommended for any learning disabled students may also help ESL students who may have a learning disability. These might include segmenting larger assignments, using color for coding or for highlighting information or permitting the student to get feedback on assignments before they are due.

Teachers with a student who is still not succeeding even when these interventions are adopted may want to resort to a volunteer tutor, but such help should be used cautiously. Although one-on-one instruction seems ideal, an untrained tutor or teacher who does not understand why the student cannot seem to learn things or requires so much review and multisensory learning opportunities can be even more frustrating to a student than a class setting.

Finally, at ELI, when an official diagnosis showed that a student had severe problems in a specific language area such as grammar or written expression, it was occasionally necessary to provide a waiver for a particular class. Although schools' policies on waivers differ widely, at ELI waivers were granted only when it was clear that not only would a class be unhelpful, but could be detrimental. Rather than ask a student to be humiliated and suffer failure again, she or he was given permission not to take the class.

◈ CONCLUSION

The LSP at ELI showed that learning disabled ESL students could be identified and helped successfully. The students in an IEP who are seriously at risk for failure, especially if they have been diagnosed with a learning disability, can profit from the same approaches to learning and language teaching and from the same accommodations afforded American students with similar language learning problems. Not only will the ESL students be aided to stay in their IEP and likely succeed in further studies, but also teachers will feel much less frustrated when they have the means to understand and help their failing students. Moreover, as Richard Beaubien of Mercer University has recently pointed out, the IEPs which can offer this support to international students, who often are not aware of learning disabilities and the assistance which learning disabled students have access to, will be doing the morally right thing (Beaubien, 1998).

◈ CONTRIBUTOR

Robin Schwarz is currently an associate lecturer in the PAL program at Curry College, in Milton, Massachusetts, in the United States. She is also a doctoral candidate in ESL and learning disabilities at Lesley University.

CHAPTER 11

Course Evaluations and Reflective Practice

Barbara Hoekje

❖ INTRODUCTION

Many intensive English Programs (IEPs) use course evaluations as a source of student feedback on the quality of teaching and extent of student learning. In fact, the American Association of Intensive English Programs (AAIEP, 2001) endorses evaluation at all levels of an IEP, including student evaluation of faculty. Feedback from the students on course evaluations serves as a source of information to the teachers and their supervisors and may be used in two major ways.

The information may be used by the supervisors with teachers in faculty reviews and other settings—an evaluative or supervisory function. Course evaluations can also be a source of student feedback to the teacher, helping the teacher understand the consequences of decisions about texts, course organization, and other aspects of the course—a developmental or formative function. These two functions are widely recognized within faculty evaluation generally. (See, e.g., the discussion in the overview of approaches to ESL faculty evaluation by Pennington & Young, 1989.)

This chapter examines the question of how information from course evaluations can best be utilized for evaluative and formative functions within an IEP. Specifically, I explore the value of teachers' reflections on final course evaluations as a source of teacher learning that not only informs teachers about their own teaching but also provides insight in supervisory conversations between teachers and administrators.

❖ CONTEXT

The English Language Center (ELC) is an IEP located at Drexel University, an urban university in the United States known for its programs in engineering, business, and design. The ELC serves about 600 students a year from a wide variety of countries in four 11-week terms, with a midterm admission in the 6th week.

The ELC specializes in academic and professional language preparation. The academic program is a six-level intensive program consisting of two core morning classes (a spoken and a written English class), from 9 am to 12 pm, and an afternoon elective class, for a total of 18 hours per week of study. The ELC program staff includes a director and associate director, along with other administrative personnel. The faculty consist of nine full-time (university auxiliary) teachers, approximately 10 part-time (university adjunct) teachers, and 7 intern instructors, who are graduate students in area MA/MS TESOL programs.

In its daily operations, the culture of the ELC reflects two powerful ideas: participatory management and reflective teaching. Participatory management refers to a philosophy of inclusion that attempts to involve major stakeholders in the decision-making process. To this end, the administrative staff meets together weekly to plan and review program activities. Faculty-run committees oversee the major areas of faculty concern, including curriculum and academic policies. There is a weekly staff meeting to discuss common areas of teaching and administrative concern. The philosophy of participatory management extends to the conception of the role of teacher in the program in that teachers are responsible for the majority of professional decisions about their work, including textbook selection and methodology within a set of curriculum guidelines overseen by a faculty committee.

Reflective teaching refers to a philosophy in which teachers take responsibility for their growth as professionals through critical reflection upon their work. The term was introduced by Schön (1983) in his book *The Reflective Practitioner* and was soon widely applied to teaching contexts, including ESL teaching (see, e.g., Bartlett, 1990; Brookfield, 1995; Richards & Lockhart, 1994). At the ELC, reflective teaching refers to a program of activities instituted with administrative support that encourages teacher reflection as a primary source of teacher learning (Hoekje, 1999; Hoekje et al., 1995). This program is the focus of this chapter, in particular, the value of teacher reflection upon course evaluations as a source of increased self-understanding on the part of the teacher as well as a source of shared information between the teacher and the supervisor.

The procedure for administering course evaluations at the ELC is the following: The instructor distributes the evaluations in class in the last week of the term, reviews the forms with the students, and then leaves the room while the students fill out the forms anonymously. Forms are returned to the directors, who read the evaluations, comment on them, and return to the instructors to read and copy for their teaching portfolios, which are submitted to the IEP directors at the end of the academic year as part of their annual reviews.

The evaluation forms were developed in a process of discussion among the faculty and the directors and are designed to elicit open-ended responses about the students' perceptions of the quality of the course and teaching, including questions on the most and least valuable part of the class; if and how the student's skills have improved; what the student liked and did not like about the instructor's teaching; which course activities were the most beneficial, and how students reacted to the textbooks and other materials in the course. The evaluations elicit verbal responses only rather than ask students to circle numbers or mark responses on a scale.

The directors review teachers' evaluations and address issues that are raised by the students, including comments on instructor punctuality, perceived prejudice against (or for) a particular nationality, timeliness in returning work, and other pedagogical issues. Teachers are accountable to the directors for student comments on the quality of the teaching and the course.

As educational researchers have pointed out, using course evaluations as a source of information to supervisors about the quality of teaching can be problematic. For one, it is not always easy to standardize administration of the forms. For example, in an IEP where students' proficiency levels range from beginning to advanced, the question of how much time to allot to administer forms is not straightforward. In addition, some teachers will inevitably review the questions more carefully and generally give the process more weight than others.

Other limitations in eliciting student responses to a course include the fact that the activities done in the last several weeks may dominate students' memories, or one negative experience may stand out over a routine of good ones. The opportunity of anonymity may lead some students to be irresponsible in their remarks, especially if they are angry at the instructor or the program in general. As Brookfield (1995) points out, evaluations can also reflect student satisfaction or comfort with the instructor rather than the quality of teaching. Although student comfort with the instructor cannot be overlooked as a valid measure in a language learning classroom, there is still the chance that instructors who are the most rigorous or ask students to do the most risk-taking may be penalized compared to instructors who adopt a more "feel good" approach. Finally, ESL students may also be uncomfortable or unfamiliar with the experience of evaluating the instructor, as Erber (1991) points out. They may lack the language skills or cultural savvy to couch their criticisms appropriately, or they may focus on what to professional educators is the wrong thing (e.g., physical attractiveness).

In their function of providing student feedback to the instructor on aspects of the course, course evaluations are also vulnerable to criticism. For one, anonymity is a problem in understanding student responses. The more teachers understand their students as individuals (as teachers are encouraged to do), the more they recognize that students respond individually to instruction, either because of their individual learning style, their role in the classroom dynamic (Ehrman & Dörnyei, 1998), or their individual adjustment due to culture shock issues and general goal satisfaction. Teachers want to know who has written a remark in order to understand it better, and often feel they cannot interpret a remark unless they know who has written it. Thus, the value of anonymous feedback to the instructor may be more limited than it is in more personal contexts, such as conferences or response journals.

Still another criticism of course evaluations as a source of information to instructors is that they are post-hoc. The instructor receives the information too late to do anything about it with this group of students—and the next group might be completely different. Other more timely ways of getting information from students— what Brookfield (1995) terms "getting inside students' heads" (p. 92), include student learning journals, regular short discussions about teaching and learning processes, and student "critical incident" reports about their learning experiences in the course. Other resources include ongoing course rating forms and narrative descriptions by students, along with observations by colleagues (Lowman, 1995). These methods contrast with final course evaluations in that they provide student feedback throughout the course, are personalized and identifiable, and link the instructor's teaching to the students' learning process.

Finally, there is the issue of how well instructors can make use of their course evaluation feedback. Many postsecondary programs (including many IEPs) rely on quantitative data that are more easily managed in aggregate or comparative form from the administrative side. However, many faculty find it difficult or unpleasant to use numbers as the basis of feedback on teaching. On the other hand, verbal comments may be ambiguous, isolated from context, or contradictory. In any case, Lowman (1995) argues that faculty will get the most out of student evaluations if they have the opportunity to review them in consultation with an experienced instructor or another source in which they have confidence in order to understand what they can do differently to improve (pp. 301–302).

In summary, the use of final course evaluations has been shown to have limitations in both its supervisory function and its formative function of providing information to instructors. Looking back to the time when I first began to see the limitations of course evaluations, it was the latter area that was of greatest concern to me. How could course evaluations be most useful to teachers? When I saw anonymous remarks that I believed might hurt the feelings of the teacher, I was tempted to take out the pages and crumple them up. From my own experience as a teacher, I was concerned that teachers would give excessive emotional power to students' critical remarks and be unable to fairly evaluate their own teaching even in the face of other positive remarks. At the same time, I did not want teachers to use a few positive or bland student comments to bless an activity that they actually suspected was pedagogically weak. Moreover, many student comments were so minimal that it was hard to understand the student's experience at all. I felt frustrated that a rich world of student experience lay untapped or inaccessible to the instructor and to me in my role of supervisor of teacher development.

Thus, I suggested to the faculty several years ago that they begin to synthesize the students' comments with their own understanding about the way the activities, texts, and teaching went with the particular group of students. I hoped that this kind of synthesis could provide a fuller record of the faculty's teaching process and could be included in their teaching portfolios. I felt at the time, and still feel, that the potential of course evaluations lay in the teacher's probing of the comments and sense making of them in light of their lived experience of teaching the course. The process of reflection would inform the process of teacher development and the supervisory conversation between teacher and administrator. Thus my own limitations in making sense out of course evaluations set the stage for including "reflecting upon final evaluations" as one of the reflective teaching activities at the ELC.

◈ DESCRIPTION
Reflective Teaching at the ELC

The program of reflective teaching activities at the ELC is a framework for the issue of faculty learning from student evaluations. Reflective teaching (RT) at the ELC refers to a set of activities that is discussed and promoted at the beginning of each teaching term and is designed to encourage teacher development through active reflective practice. In contrast to the more formal teacher development program given once per term (Staff Development Day) at which speakers present information about a topic in a full-group setting, RT activities are more localized, individual, and personal. Participation is voluntary and ebbs and flows through the year. Reports of the activities are not required unless participants want reimbursement for incurred expenses, in which case they must attach a brief summary of the topic of the RT activity along with their requests for reimbursement. On the other hand, the directors encourage teachers who have participated in RT activities to write about them for their teaching portfolios as evidence of interest in teaching development.

During the 5 years of the program, I have received about 75 summaries of participation in RT activities. The most popular choice of RT activity is the discussion of teaching with one or two colleagues, with peer classroom observation being the least chosen activity. Several larger groups of teachers have met together to discuss special topics such as the teaching of writing or pronunciation. Teachers have also met to develop their portfolios or discuss how to frame teaching issues for conference presentation. The set of RT activities can vary from term to term, but usually includes these staples:

1. intern mentoring (an activity in which the experienced instructor observes and discusses issues with an intern)

2. reflection upon classroom teaching through writing or discussion with colleagues

3. reflection on final evaluations through writing or discussion

4. classroom observations among peers and follow-up discussion

Instructors who want to pursue new RT activities (i.e., not previously tried) are always encouraged to do so.

❖ DISTINGUISHING FEATURES
Teachers' Reflections on Course Evaluations

In this section, I draw upon 11 reports submitted over several years as a means to illustrate the power of the reflective process. These reports represent the work of 10 different instructors, 6 full-time, 2 adjunct, and 2 intern instructors (one full-time instructor wrote two reports). Two of these reports described the teachers' discussions with others about their evaluations, whereas the other nine were reflections written by individual teachers. In their reflections, the instructors considered a wide variety of topics, including classic issues of practitioner reflection, such as teacher's role, pedagogical decision-making issues, and teaching philosophy.

One report was of a discussion between an intern and an experienced instructor held at the intern's request to review his evaluations. The intern had received confusing student comments to the effect that he needed to "concentrate the students' attention" in class. The seasoned instructor discussed some of the different possible interpretations with the intern, including time management and information presentation issues. Thus the remarks became the springboard for a useful exploration of possible classroom responses.

The other selections discussed here are reflections written by teachers about their own evaluations. Excerpt 1 is a reflection written by a teacher who had experimented with aspects of her course and wanted to do her own synthesis in light of the students' comments. She wrote:

> 1. I wanted to reflect on this term's written class and the course evaluations because I tried some new things this term. I don't think that I will be able to meet with a group for discussion, but I wanted to take the time to write out some thoughts about the class and the student comments. I'd like to tell you about some of the things that I tried and respond to the final evaluations. I would welcome any comments that you have about these reflections and the activities that I describe.

It is worth noting that the teacher in Excerpt 1 has written her thoughts directly to me as the teaching supervisor while she reflects on her evaluations. Although I am not always explicitly named as the audience, the writing in the individual reflections on evaluations is often dialogic in nature as the teacher shares with me his or her observations of the work as well as comes to a deeper understanding of it personally. In some cases, teachers are writing to answer questions the director or I have explicitly posed. In Excerpt 2, for example, I had written to the teacher, "Some mixed reviews on texts—would you use them again?" In her answer, the instructor clarified her understanding of why the students might have disliked the text, bringing into focus issues of learning style and learning strategies, which are important pedagogical considerations for language teachers:

> 2. I like the reading text a lot and would use it again. I think the problem is that students expect to understand everything and they're just not going to. I tried to teach them that it's not a good strategy to try to understand every single word, but that is very difficult for students to accept. . . . The writing text I think is pretty good, but none of the Level Four ones are ideal. At least this one has examples of essay, which many of them don't, and fairly useful integrated grammar. . . . I'm open to suggestions of new/better texts.

In other cases, the teacher is simply sharing with me the inside story of his or her teaching. In Excerpt 3, the teacher reflects upon the teacher's role in the classroom in relation to the pedagogical issue of how to give students more opportunities to speak in class. Her questions seem to be working in two ways—rhetorically, as a way for the teacher herself to define an action research agenda related to these issues, and functionally, as a request to me for some suggestions or help:

> 3. Some students thought I spoke too much, didn't give them enough chances to speak and enough feedback. How do I give the students more chances to speak in class? I tried to give the students opportunities to speak every day by doing group or pair work. During class discussions, I tend to do a lot of talking. Students have a tendency to ask me information questions about US culture and life, and I tend to answer them. How do I get away from being the expert/authority?

In another case, the instructor took the opportunity to ponder the meaning of the term *professional* as students had used it:

> 4. Another aspect of the evaluations that struck me as interesting is the mention of the word "professional" in reference to me as a teacher. I find myself wondering about this word choice. What is it that students are really commenting on when they say that I am professional? My guess is that it has something to do with my extensive experience in the ESL writing classroom. However, I also think that it relates to my philosophy of teaching.
>
> My philosophy of teaching in general is based on the belief that knowledge is created through an interaction between the expertise of the teacher and the individual knowledge and experiences of the students, that doing is essential to learning, and that learning is facilitated by a student-teacher relationship built on respect and kindness. Students in my classrooms receive frequent and substantial individual attention, and I try to create a classroom atmosphere that is inclusive and friendly, yet formal.

In this case, the teacher overtly linked the use of a positive adjective to a philosophy of teaching rather than an expert methodology or set of classroom activities. In so doing, she may have clarified it for herself for the first time. This entry demonstrates the value to teachers of probing the basis of positive remarks rather than just basking in their glow.

In some reflections, the teachers simply review the course for themselves in light of the students' comments. They may use the information to make decisions about course planning, as in the following example:

> 5. During the course, I incorporated vocabulary activities, projects, and movies with the listening tasks. The students stated that they really enjoyed the vocabulary activities and that these vocabulary exercises were also quite useful for them. As a result, I will continue to enhance the lectures with vocabulary activities before students listen, as a preview, and after, as a review.

In another case, an intern teaching a beginning pronunciation course evaluated her experience, noting how important group dynamics were to the classroom atmosphere and how certain full-group activities supported these dynamics:

> 6. I think the single most important contribution to the classroom atmosphere was the group work done as an entire class. I remember the first activity like this was interesting. One student was supposed to call on another, ask them something, and then that person would ask someone else, etc. Most of the students did not know their classmates' names, and so there was a lot of pointing, trying to pronounce each person's name, moments of awkwardness, that eventually turned to laughter. I think having these class activities occasionally really helped to keep the class together. By the end of the term, I felt like the students generally knew and cared about their classmates and their progress.

One aspect of the reports that I especially value as the supervisor of instruction is the identification of problems and issues that faculty face in their teaching that I am not aware of. Many teachers do come to talk to me about ongoing issues, but many do not, either because they do not want the supervisor to know about them or because they may not understand or recognize the issues themselves in a way they can talk about them as they are happening. When I get reports such as the following, however, I get a clear picture of the teacher's experience from the inside:

> 7. I had a problem with three non-traditional students, who made me uncomfortable. One student (who is a professor in his country) took up too much air time and gave me advice on how to teach the class in front of other students. Another student (who is a psychologist) would say anything that was on her mind and make negative comments about class topics and activities—e.g., this topic is hard to discuss, or this activity is too easy or boring, etc. How should I have responded to that? And the third student would sit in class and talk to another student while someone else was speaking. I felt like no matter what I did, I couldn't please these high-maintenance students.

This is an intriguing selection because one can see in it some of the reasons teaching in an IEP can be difficult for teachers. First, some students who come to the program are more demanding to have in class than other students, either because they are older (or younger) than others, more (or less) professionally oriented than other students in the class, or from a culture with very different classroom norms of behavior. Students in IEPs may also be suffering from culture shock, which can lead to difficult behavior in the classroom as they seek to establish their former authority or build friendships. Reading this report reminded me that dealing with challenging students and establishing positive group dynamics is a core issue for teachers, though it surfaces in different ways in their classrooms. Through these reports, I am able to have a more informed understanding of some teaching issues that concern the faculty.

The next example, which I discuss at some length, illustrates this point. It comes from a detailed, six-page reflection from an instructor probing a set of issues in an advanced writing course, including the nature of grammar instruction in an upper level writing class. This issue has a long history in our program: Students usually want grammar, yet often resist its instruction as tedious or redundant. Having received some negative comments about his grammar instruction in his course, this experienced teacher found himself trying to trace how this issue played out in his writing class. In his comments, the instructor underscores the issue of new versus renewing students in the program and relates classroom decisions to a changing conception of teacher's role:

> 8. I'd received enough comments against explicit grammar instruction from students in the spring (all were renewing students), as well as before, that I thought I shouldn't make grammar a significant part of the class—at least not of my own initiative. This ties in with a general shift I've been making in my teaching approach for upper levels: to "push" less in terms of what I decide students should do and allow more "pull" from them—to lead students up to that point where they feel positive about requesting individual work that they themselves recognize as being beneficial. . . . Thus, I decided that for the summer term we would instead do more reading and vocabulary development than before and less teacher-initiated grammar. Once the summer term started (with all new students, by the way), I did discuss with individual students the grammar problems in their writing, as I always do, and I encouraged and took individual questions about grammar in the class whenever students had them—and they often did. I also mentioned that we could spend more time on formal grammar study if they were interested.

The teacher describes the students' response to this approach, as expressed to him in the midterm conference, and explains the impact upon his class of the midterm arrivals:

> Then during midterm conferences, nearly every student made clear to me that they wanted more grammar instruction in class, and I agreed to provide it. Indeed, some students even indicated that that's what they always expected me, as their writing teacher, to do. Then the next day, with summer midterm arrivals, the class size more than doubled, and there were actually more midterm arrivals than term-initial students. As luck would have it, most of these midterm arrivals were uncommonly versed in English grammar. In fact, one was a practicing teacher of English in her own country and two others were English teachers-in-training in theirs.

He notes that he changed his approach to the instruction of grammar in the following way:

> My way of handling the situation was to delve into some formal grammar study but frequently check student reactions along the way. By doing this, I was able to tell that some of the material could be condensed or not done at all, while more intricate or less frequently studied points could get attention.

Finally, he addresses the course evaluations he had received, which included a set of negative comments about his handling of grammar in the class:

> Still, the results were that five of the eight student evaluations had a comment that we had studied more grammar than necessary. Examples:
>
> 1. "He'd better cut off detailed or easy grammars."
> 2. "We spent too much time on simple grammar questions."
> 3. "Some grammar that I had already known (I believe they were quite useful for others)."
>
> On the other hand, two of the eight stated:
>
> 1. "I would like to have less essay structure and more grammar and vocabulary."
> 2. "The first classes I needed the necessity to study more grammar and we ask the teacher. After, my classmates and I felt that the classes became more interesting. Really I'm very satisfied."

The instructor goes on to pursue the issue of the which-grammar-and-how-to-teach-it problem at this level. The excerpts already cited here demonstrate that the instructor has far more information about the conflicting issues in this question than someone outside the class would, even knowing the general issues in our program. Unfortunately, reading student comments such as "He'd better cut off detailed or easy grammars" does not help the supervisor understand the dynamics in his classroom or the level of attention the issue has already received by the instructor.

Of course, simply the fact that an instructor is conscious of the dynamics of an issue does not mean he or she has been able to handle them as successfully as possible. It does mean that if I am to have anything worth saying to a teacher about his or her classroom, having the inside story on the classroom helps us both have a place to begin. In the case here, it is very useful to our discussion that the instructor has identified as clearly as he has some important dynamics worth exploring: expectations of new versus renewing students; a testing and placement process that groups students with divergent grammar backgrounds in the same class; a curriculum that backgrounds grammar in favor of production in writing; and so on.

This teacher's reflection also shows how teachers have to cope with administrative decisions (e.g., admission of a large group of midterm students) that have pedagogical consequences that may surface on teachers' evaluations. How can or should this instructor's experience be used to provide feedback on administrative decisions such as the structure of classes and the nature of the curriculum? I see my role as teaching supervisor as one that includes the responsibility of distilling and summarizing the classroom experiences of many individual teachers in order to better inform programmatic decision making at the ELC.

To summarize, this section has given examples from teachers' reflections on their course evaluations to show the kinds of issues to which teachers have responded, including conceptions of the teacher's and student's role, philosophy of teaching, and other core issues in a professional's approach to his or her work. The position was taken that even individually written reflections can be understood as part of a conversation about teaching with me as the audience. In this regard, the teacher's reflections can be seen as responding to and informing the developmental and evaluative dimensions of course evaluations in the IEP.

◈ PRACTICAL IDEAS

The purpose of this chapter has been to describe a program that can be instituted by the administrators of an IEP that allows substantial freedom of choice and local initiation by instructors. In particular, the value of this program for reflecting on final course evaluations was emphasized. The following suggestions may be useful to others interested in establishing a program of this sort.

Promote the Program as a Voluntary, Teacher-Owned Resource

RT activities are a local, individualized form of teacher development, in which a teacher's learning can only result from his or her willingness to be involved and invested in the activity. Because investment cannot be mandated, only encouraged, the program is most successful when voluntarily elected. However, there will be times when a supervisor might request that a teacher do a reflection (e.g., on course evaluations as in the case study described in this chapter) to achieve greater insight or understanding. I believe this will be an effective resource to the extent that teachers are familiar with the benefits of reflective teaching in ongoing, voluntary activities.

Provide Options and Flexibility

Provide options to the faculty for RT activities. This chapter has focused on the value of reflection in understanding course evaluations, but there are many other possible ways to use RT activities in an IEP, including observing other teachers' classes and discussing them with them, meeting with another teacher to talk about classroom dynamics with shared students, or meeting as a small group of teachers to reflect on teaching philosophies and how they manifest themselves in the classroom. Provide ideas for individual activities as well as paired or small group collaborations and give teachers the flexibility to define their own topics.

Provide Administrative Support

Support the program administratively by providing logistical and financial support for RT activities as the budget allows. Free teachers up from other responsibilities to participate in the activities, providing substitutes when necessary so that they can observe other teachers. The cost of the program (lunches, substitutes) is minimal compared to paying for speakers or larger scale staff luncheons. If necessary, limit participation in certain events or set reimbursement limits.

Treat Teacher Involvement Seriously

Count teacher involvement as serious evidence of interest in teaching development for the purposes of annual review, portfolio development, or recommendations. Participation in RT activities is one way that teachers can demonstrate their interest and involvement in improving teaching, especially when done on a voluntary basis. Supervisors should discuss with their faculty in advance the way that participation in RT activities will be counted in any review.

Allow Privacy in Reporting on RT Activities

Teachers should be free to explore the dynamics of their teaching honestly and fully without fear of supervisory inspection. For those seeking reimbursement for lunches, and other such activities, tie reimbursement to brief written summaries of the topic of the RT activity rather than the specific content itself.

◈ CONCLUSION

As I have continued to discuss the issue of course evaluations with the ELC faculty, it has become clearer to me that course evaluations are only one place to seek systematic student feedback on the courses and teaching, and probably not the best one at that. If one asks "How can I get information about my teaching?" there are many places to look for answers, such as peer observations, videotaping, student learning journals and conferences. But accountability to students at the IEP is important as well, and course evaluations have a well-established niche as a means for providing this accountability in most postsecondary educational settings.

At the ELC, as in other IEPs, the process of improving course evaluations to serve student accountability and teacher development is ongoing. For example, the Academic Affairs Committee has recently examined the course evaluation process at the ELC and recommended several changes, including the addition of student self-assessment questions to describe the student's contribution to the course in terms of time and effort spent. However well-worded these questions are, the full potential of the feedback is only realized when the instructor invests time and critical thought in examining this information in light of his or her lived experience of teaching. What administrators can offer is institutional support for teachers who engage in this process as a primary source of teacher learning within a professional practice community.

◈ CONTRIBUTOR

Barbara Hoekje is associate director of the English Language Center at Drexel University, in Pennsylvania, in the United States. She also teaches courses in ESL humanities, linguistics, and intercultural communication in the Department of Humanities and Communications.

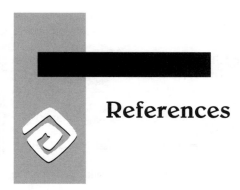

References

American Association of Intensive English Programs. (2001). Retrieved May 17, 2001, from http://www.aaiep.org/

Bailey, K. M. (1998). *Learning about language assessment: Dilemmas, decisions, and directions.* Pacific Grove, CA: Heinle & Heinle.

Bartlett, L. (1990). Teacher development through reflective teaching. In J. Richards & D. Nunan (Eds.), *Second language teacher education* (pp. 202–214). Cambridge: Cambridge University Press.

Beaubien, R. (1998). *Adult learning disabilities in intensive English programs: A call for action.* Paper presented at the 33rd Annual TESOL Convention, New York, NY.

Beebe, L. M. (1983). Risk-taking and the language learner. In H. W. Selinger & M. H. Long (Eds.), *Classroom oriented research in second language acquisition* (pp. 39–66). Rowley, MA: Newbury House.

Benesch, S. (2001). *Critical English for academic purposes: Theory, politics and practice.* Mahwah, NJ: Lawrence Erlbaum.

Benson, P. J., & Heidish, P. (1995). The ESL technical expert: Writing processes and classroom practices. In D. Belcher & G. Braine (Eds.), *Academic writing: Essays on research and pedagogy* (pp. 313–330). Norwood, NJ: Ablex.

Berkenkotter, C., & Huckin, T. N. (1995). *Genre knowledge in disciplinary communication: Cognition/culture/power.* Hillsdale, NJ: Lawrence Erlbaum.

Brinton, D. M., Snow, M. A., & Wesche, M. (1989). *Content-based second language instruction.* New York: Harper Collins.

Brookfield, S. (1995). *Becoming a critically reflective teacher.* San Francisco: Jossey-Bass.

Brooks, E. (1988). When there are no links between ESL and content courses. In S. Benesch (Ed.), *Ending remediation: Linking ESL and content in higher education* (pp. 21–32). Washington, DC: TESOL.

Cargill, M., Cadman, K., & McGowan, U. (2001). Postgraduate writing: Using intersecting genres in a collaborative, content-based program. In I. Leki (Ed.), *Academic writing programs.* Alexandria, VA: TESOL.

Carkin, S. (1997). Language program leadership as intercultural management. In M. A. Christison & F. L. Stoller (Eds.), *A handbook for language program administrators* (pp. 49–60). Burlingame, CA: Alta.

Carr, W., & Kemmis, S. (1986). *Becoming critical: Education, knowledge, and action research.* London: Falmer Press.

Chamot, A. U., Barnhardt, S., El-Dinary, P. B., & Robbins, J. (1999). *The learning strategies handbook.* White Plains, NY: Addison Wesley Longman.

Christison, M. A., & Stoller, F. L. (Eds.). (1997). *A handbook for language program administrators.* Burlingame, CA: Alta.

Clandinin, D. J., Davies, A., Hogan, P., & Kennard, B. (Eds.). (1993). *Learning to teach, teaching to learn: Stories of collaboration in teacher education.* New York: Teachers College Press.

Clarke, M., Davis, A., Rhodes, L. K., & Baker, E. D. (1998). Principles of collaboration in school-university partnerships. *TESOL Quarterly, 32,* 592–600.

Cole, A. L., & Knowles, J. G. (2000). *Researching teaching: Exploring teacher development through reflexive inquiry.*Boston: Allyn & Bacon.

Colorado State University. (1999). *Welcome to the Intensive English Program.* Retrieved July 23, 2001, from http://www.colostate.edu/Depts/IEP/

Commission on English Language Program Accreditation. (n.d.). Retrieved May 17, 2001, from http://www.cea-accredit.org/

Crandall, J. A. (Ed.). (1987). *ESL through content-area instruction: Mathematics, science, and social studies.* McHenry, IL: Delta Systems.

Crandall, J. A., Dale, T. C., Rhodes, N. C., & Spanos, G. A. (1988). The language of mathematics: The English barrier. In A. LaBarca & L. M. Bailey (Eds.), *Issues in L2: Theory as practice/Practice as theory* (pp. 129–150). Norwood, NJ: Ablex. (Reprinted from *Issues in College Learning Centers,* 7, 13–40)

Cummins, J. (1979). Linguistic interdependence and the educational development of bilingual children. *Review of Educational Research, 49,* 222–251.

Cummins, J. (1996). *Negotiating identities: Education for empowerment in a diverse society.* Ontario, CA: California Association for Bilingual Education.

Dantas-Whitney, M. (1998). The discovery project. *TESOL Journal, 7*(4), 37–38.

Dantas-Whitney, M., & Larson, A. (1996 August/September). Minisheltered courses: Authentic university preparation for intermediate students. *TESOL Matters,* p. 9.

Dantas-Whitney, M., & Larson, A. (2000). Exploring the balance between student autonomy and teacher direction. *ThaiTESOL Bulletin, 13*(1), 1–7.

Deckert, G. D. (1993). Perspectives on plagiarism from ESL students in Hong Kong. *Journal of Second Language Writing, 2*(2), 131–148.

Dinklage, K. (1998). *Regarding college students' inability to learn a foreign language.* Paper presented at the Inaugural International Conference on Dyslexia in Ottawa, Canada.

Dong, Y. R. (1998). Non-native graduate students' thesis/dissertation writing in science: Self-reports by students and their advisors from two U.S. institutions. *English for Specific Purposes, 17*(4), 369–390.

Dowling, B., & McDougal, M. (1990). *Change in ESL programs: Proactive or reactive?* Paper presented at the 24th Annual TESOL Convention, San Francisco, CA.

Downey, D. (1992). *Accommodating learning disabled students in foreign language classes.* Paper presented at the Conference on Foreign Language Learning and Learning Disabilities, American University, Washington, DC.

Dudley-Evans, T. (1994). Genre analysis: An approach to text analysis for ESP. In M. Coulthard (Ed.), *Advances in written text analysis* (pp. 219–228). New York: Routledge.

Dudley-Evans, T. (1995). Common-core and specific approaches to the teaching of academic writing. In D. Belcher & G. Braine, (Eds.), *Academic writing: Essays on research and pedagogy* (pp. 293–312). Norwood, NJ: Ablex.

Ehrman, M., & Dörnyei, Z. (1998). *Interpersonal dynamics in second language education.* Thousand Oaks, CA: Sage.

Erber, N. (1991). Student bias in teacher evaluations. In *Improving learning in ESL through research: Teachers and students as researchers* (Papers from the 1991 ESL Council Conference). New York: City University of New York, Instructional Resource Center, Office of Academic Affairs.

Eskey, D. (1997). The IEP as a nontraditional entity. In M. A. Christison & F. Stoller (Eds.), *A handbook for language program administrators* (pp. 21–30). Burlingame, CA: Alta.

‌

Esposito, M., Marshall, K., & Stoller, F. L. (1997). Poster sessions by experts. In D. M. Brinton & P. Master (Eds.), *New ways in content-based instruction* (pp. 115–118). Alexandria, VA: TESOL.

Eyraud, K., Giles, G., Koenig, S., & Stoller, F. L. (2000). The word wall approach: A means for promoting L2 vocabulary learning. *English Teaching Forum, 38,* 2–11.

Fanselow, J. (1977). Beyond *Rashomon*: Conceptualizing and describing the teaching act. *TESOL Quarterly, 11,* 17–41.

Ferris, D. (1998). Students' views of academic aural/oral skills: A comparative needs analysis. *TESOL Quarterly, 32,* 289–318.

Flaitz, J., Feyten, C., Fox, S., & Mukherjee, K. (1995). Raising general awareness of language learning strategies: A little bit goes a long way. *Hispania, 78*(2), 337–348.

Flowerdew, J. (1993). An educational, or process, approach to the teaching of professional genres. *English Language Teaching Journal, 47*(4), 305–316.

Freeman, D. (1998). *Doing teacher research: From inquiry to understanding.* Pacific Grove, CA: Heinle & Heinle.

Freeman, D., & Johnson, K. (1998). Reconceptualizing the knowledge-base of language teacher education. *TESOL Quarterly, 32,* 397–417.

Ganschow, L., & Sparks, R. (1995). Effects of direct instruction in Spanish phonology on the native-language skills and foreign language aptitude of at-risk foreign language learners. *Journal of Learning Disabilities, 28*(2), 107–117.

Gebhard, J., & Oprandy, R. (1999). *Language teaching awareness: A guide to exploring beliefs and practices.* New York: Cambridge University Press.

Gee, J. P. (1990). *Social linguistics and literacies: Ideology in discourses.* New York: Falmer Press.

Gerber, P. (1998). Characteristics of adults with specific learning disabilities. In M. A. Corley, K. Lenz, & N. Sturomski, (Eds.), *Serving adults with learning disabilities: Implications for effective practice* (pp.1–12). Washington, DC: United States Department of Education.

Golombek, P. R. (1998). A study of language teachers? Personal practical knowledge. *TESOL Quarterly, 32,* 447–464.

Goodlad, J. I. (1994). *Educational renewal: Better teachers, better schools.* San Francisco: Jossey-Bass.

Grabe, W., Stoller, F. L., & Tardy, C. (2000). Disciplinary knowledge as a foundation for teacher preparation. In J. K. Hall & W. Eggington (Eds.), *The sociopolitics of English language teaching* (pp. 178–194). Clevedon, England: Multilingual Matters.

Hafernik, J. J., & Burgamy, R. M. (1985, October). ESL on campus: Who gets credit? *CATESOL News,* 5.

Henry, J. (1995). *If not now: Developmental readers in the college classroom.* Portsmouth, NH: Boynton/Cook.

Herbert, J., & Reppen, R. (1999). Selecting and evaluating TOEFL material. *TESOL Journal, 8*(4), 41–43.

Hicks, D. (Ed.). (1996). *Discourse, learning, and schooling.* New York: Cambridge University Press.

Hoekje, B. (1999). Teacher conversations as professional socialization. *Journal of Intensive English Programs, 13,* 1–18.

Hoekje, B., Marrecau, A., McVey, D., Schlatter, R., Swartley, E., & Williams, H. (1995). *Teachers keeping journals: Reflecting on our work.* Paper presented at the 28th Annual TESOL Convention, Long Beach, CA.

Hyland, K. (1997). Scientific claims and community values: Articulating an academic culture. *Language and Communication, 17*(1), 19–31.

Hyon, S. (1996). Genre in three traditions: Implications for ESL. *TESOL Quarterly, 30,* 693–722.

Ijiri, L., & Rooney, G. (1995). Learning disabilities in speakers of English as a second language. In J. U. Adelizzi & D. B. Goss (Eds.), *A closer look: Practitioners' perspectives and reflections on post-secondary LD education*. Milton, MA: Curry College.

Institute of Languages (Producer). (1994). *The PPP paradigm in contemporary teaching contexts*. [Video]. Sydney, Australia: University of New South Wales.

Jacoby, S., Leech, D., & Holten, C. (1995). A genre-based developmental writing course for undergraduate ESL science majors. In D. Belcher & G. Braine, (Eds.). *Academic writing: Essays on research and pedagogy* (pp. 351–373). Norwood, NJ: Ablex.

Jenks, F. L. (1997). The quest for academic legitimacy: Building for language program entry into institutional and community infrastructures. In M. A. Christison & F. L. Stoller (Eds.), *A handbook for language program administrators* (pp. 107–121). Burlingame, CA: Alta.

Johns, A. M. (1992). Academic English: What can we do? *Journal of Intensive English Studies, 6*(Fall), 61–69.

Johnson, K. (1996). The role of theory in L2 teacher education. *TESOL Quarterly, 30*, 765–771.

Kaplan, R. B. (1997). An IEP is a many-splendored thing. In M. A. Christison & F. L. Stoller (Eds.), *A handbook for language program administrators* (pp. 3–19). Burlingame, CA: Alta.

Kay, H., & Dudley-Evans, T. (1998). Genre: What teachers think. *English Language Teaching Journal, 52*(4), 308–314.

Lambert, W. E., & Tucker, G. R. (1972). *Bilingual education of children: The St. Lambert experience*. Rowley, MA: Newbury House.

Larsen-Freeman, D. (1986). *Techniques and principles in language teaching*. Oxford: Oxford University Press.

Larsen-Freeman, D. (1999, November). *The role of grammar in a communicative approach*. Workshop presentation, University of South Florida, Tampa.

Lave, J., & Wenger, E. (1991). *Situated learning: Legitimate peripheral participation*. Cambridge: Cambridge University Press.

Leki, I. (Ed.). (2001). *Academic writing programs*. Alexandria, VA: TESOL.

Leki, I., & Carson, J. (1997). "Completely different worlds": EAP and the writing experiences of ESL students in university courses. *TESOL Quarterly, 31*, 39–69.

Long, M. (1983). Does second language instruction make a difference? A review of research. *TESOL Quarterly, 17*, 359–382.

Lortie, D. (1975). *Schoolteacher: A sociological study*. Chicago: University of Chicago Press.

Lowman, J. (1995). *Mastering the techniques of teaching* (2nd ed.). San Francisco: Jossey-Bass.

Mach, T., & Stoller, F. L. (1997). Synthesizing content on a continuum. In D. M. Brinton & P. Master (Eds.), *New ways in content-based instruction* (pp. 61–63). Alexandria, VA: TESOL.

Mach, T., Stoller, F. L., & Tardy, C. (1997). A gambit-driven debate. In D. M. Brinton & P. Master (Eds.), *New ways in content-based instruction* (pp. 64–68). Alexandria, VA: TESOL.

The Macquarie Dictionary (2nd ed.). (1991). Sydney, Australia: Macquarie Library.

Maggio, M., & Gay, C. (1986). Intercultural communication as an integral part of an ESL program: The University of Southern California experience. In P. Byrd (Ed.), *Teaching across cultures in the university ESL program* (pp. 93–98). Washington, DC: NAFSA.

Martino, M. (1992). Issues in ESL: Give credit where credit is due. *College ESL, 2*(1), 20–23.

Mayher, J. S., Lester, N. B., & Pradl, G. M. (1983). *Learning to write/writing to learn*. Portsmouth, NH: Boynton/Cook.

Monash University. (1999). *Monash University: Leading the way*. Melbourne, Australia: Author.

Moulton, M. R., & Holmes, V. L. (2000). An ESL capstone course: Integrating research tools, techniques, and technology. *TESOL Journal, 9*(2), 23–29.

National Information Center for Children and Youth with Disabilities (NICHCY). (2001). General information about learning disabilities. (Fact Sheet No. 7). Retrieved May 17, 2001, from http://www.nichcy.org/pubs/factshe/fs7txt.htm

Nixon, U. (1996). Adjusting to Australia: Insights from student journals in a TESOL program. *Prospect, 11*(3), 29–44,

Nunan, D. (1991). Communicative tasks and the language curriculum. *TESOL Quarterly, 25,* 279–295.

Nunan, D. (1992). *Research methods in language learning.* Cambridge: Cambridge University Press.

Nunan, D. (1998). Encouraging learner independence. In J. Reid (Ed.), *Understanding learning styles in the second language classroom* (pp. 147–155). Upper Saddle River, NJ: Prentice Hall Regents.

Ortiz, A., Robertson-Courtney, P., & Wilkinson, C. Y. (1990). *AIM for the BEST: Assessment and intervention model for the bilingual exceptional student.* Arlington, VA: Development Associates.

Pavesi, M. (1986). Markedness, discoursal modes, and relative clause formation in a formal and an informal context. *Studies in Second Language Acquisition, 8*(1), 38–55.

Pennington, M., & Young, A. (1989). Approaches to faculty evaluation for ESL. *TESOL Quarterly, 23,* 619–646.

Perkins, K., & Larsen-Freeman, D. (1975). The effect of formal instruction on the order of morpheme acquisition. *Language Learning, 25*(2), 237–243.

Peters, T. J., & Waterman, R. H. (1982). *In search of excellence.* New York: Warner.

Pica, T. (1983). Adult acquisition of English as a second language under different conditions of exposure. *Language Learning, 33*(4), 465–497.

Pica, T. (1985). The selective impact of classroom instruction on second language acquisition. *Applied Linguistics, 6*(3), 214–222.

Pienemann, M. (1984). Psychological constraints on the teachability of languages. *Studies in Second Language Acquisition, 6*(2), 186–214.

Porter, P. A., Goldstein, L. M., Leatherman, J., & Conrad, S. (1990). An ongoing dialogue: Learning logs for teacher preparation. In J. C. Richards & D. Nunan (Eds.), *Second language teacher education* (pp. 227–242). Cambridge: Cambridge University Press.

Posteguillo, S. (1999). The schematic structure of computer science research articles. *English for Specific Purposes, 18*(2), 139–160.

Richards, J., & Lockhart, C. (1994). *Reflective teaching in second language classrooms.* Cambridge: Cambridge University Press.

Rooney, G., & Schwarz, R. (1999). Learning disabled ESL students in the college setting. *Advising Quarterly, 50,* 9–16.

Rubin, J., & Thompson, I. (1982). *How to be a more successful learner.* New York: Heinle & Heinle.

Schmidt, R. (1990). The role of consciousness in second language learning. *Applied Linguistics, 11*(2), 129–158.

Schön, D. (1983). *The reflective practitioner.* New York: Basic Books.

Schwarz, R., & Terrill, L. (2000). ESL instruction and adults with learning disabilities. *ERIC Digest* (No. EDO-LE-00-01). Washington, DC: National Center for ESL Literacy Education. Retrieved May 17, 2001, from http://www.cal.org/ncle/digests/LD2.htm

Sengupta, S., Forey, G., & Hamp-Lyons, L. (1999). Supporting effective English communication within the context of teaching and research in a tertiary institute: Developing a genre model for consciousness raising. *English for Specific Purposes, 18,* S7–S22.

Shrum, J. L., & Glisan, E. W. (1994). *Teacher's handbook: Contextualized language instruction.* Boston: Heinle & Heinle.

Smith-Murdock, R. (1997). Outreach on and off campus. In M. A. Christison & F. L. Stoller (Eds.), *A handbook for language program administrators* (pp. 161–174). Burlingame, CA: Alta.

Snow, M. A., & Brinton, D. M. (1997). *The content-based classroom: Perspectives on integrating language and content.* White Plains, NY: Addison Wesley Longman.

Spanos, G. A., & Crandall, J. A. (1990). Language and problem solving. In A. M. Padilla, H. H. Fairchild, & C. M. Valadez (Eds.), *Bilingual education: Issues and strategies* (pp. 157–170). Newbury Park, CA: Sage.

Spanos, G. A., Rhodes, N. C., Dale, T. C., & Crandall, J. A. (1988). Linguistic features of mathematical problem solving: Insights and applications. In R. R. Cocking & J. P. Mestre (Eds.), *Linguistic and cultural influences on learning mathematics* (pp. 221–240). Hillsdale, NJ: Lawrence Erlbaum.

Sparks, R., Ganschow, L., & Javorsky, J. (1992). Diagnosing and accommodating the foreign language learning difficulties of college students with learning disabilities. *Learning Disabilities Research and Practice, 7,* 150–160.

Staczek, J. J., & Carkin, S. J. (1984). Intensive English programs fit in traditional academic settings: Practice and promise. In P. Larson, E. Judd, & D. S. Messerschmitt (Eds.), *On TESOL '84: A brave new world for TESOL* (pp. 289–300). Washington, DC: TESOL.

Stake, R. E. (1995). *The art of case study research.* Thousand Oaks, CA: Sage.

Stoller, F. (1994). The inviolable core of intensive English programs. *Intensive English Programs Newsletter, 12,* 1–5.

Stoller, F. (1997). The catalyst for change and innovation. In M. A. Christison & F. L. Stoller (Eds.), *A handbook for language program administrators* (pp. 33–48). Burlingame, CA: Alta.

Stoller, F. L. (1999). Time for a change: A hybrid curriculum for EAP programs. *TESOL Journal, 8*(1), 9–13.

Stoller, F. L., & Christison, M. A. (1994). Challenges for IEP administrators: Liaison with senior-level administrators and faculty development. *TESOL Journal, 3*(3), 16–20.

Stoller, F. L., Hodges, R., & Kimbrough, J. (1995). Examining the value of conversation partner programs. *Applied Language Learning, 6,* 1–12.

Stoller, F. L., White, M., & Wong, P. (1998). Motivating reluctant students in an EAP program. In J. C. Richards (Ed.), *Teaching in action: Case studies from second language classrooms* (pp. 150–154). Alexandria, VA: TESOL.

Stoynoff, S. (1989). Successfully implementing educational change and innovation. *ORTESOL Journal, 10,* 17–33.

Swales, J. M. (1990). *Genre analysis: English in academic and research settings.* Cambridge: Cambridge University Press.

Tarone, E., & Yule, G. (1989). *Focus on the language learner: Approaches to identifying and meeting the needs of second language learners.* New York: Oxford University Press.

Ur, P. (1996). *A course in language teaching.* Cambridge: Cambridge University Press.

Van Meter, J. (1990). Academic credit for ESL classes? *Review of Research in Developmental Education, 8,* 4–5. (ERIC Accession No. ED 354 961)

Vuko, E. P. (1997, March 31). In learning, the eyes have it. *Washington Post,* p. D5.

Weeks, W. H., Pederson, P. B., & Brislin, R. W. (Eds.). (1979). *A manual of structured experiences for cross-cultural learning.* Yarmouth, ME: Intercultural Press.

Weissberg, R., & Buker, S. (1990). *Writing up research: Experimental research report writing for students of English.* Englewood Cliffs, NJ: Prentice Hall Regents.

Westwood, M. (1990). Academic achievement and social adaptation among international students: A comparison groups study of the peer-pairing program. *International Journal of Intercultural Relations, 14,* 251–263.

Worthen, J. (1991, August/September). Flood tide for international education. *NAFSA Newsletter,* 12–13.

Yin, R. K. (1994). *Case study research: Design and methods* (2nd ed.). Thousand Oaks, CA: Sage.

Zamel, V. (1991). Acquiring language, literacy, and academic discourse: Entering ever new conversations. *College ESL, 1,* 10–18.

Zimmerman, D., & Rodrigues, D. (1992). *Research and writing in the disciplines.* Fort Worth, TX: Harcourt Brace Jovanovich.

Index

Note: Page numbers followed by letters
f and *t* refer to figures and tables,
respectively.

A

AAIEP. *See* American Association of
  Intensive English Programs
Academic skills, seminar in, 15–16
Academic survival skills, for learning
  disabled ESL students, 126, 128
Academy for Educational Development
  (AED), 77, 79
Accommodations, for learning disabled ESL
  students, 132
Accountability to students, 145
Accreditation, of IEPs, 1, 110
Acculturation
  of students, to U.S. academic demands,
     78, 79, 80, 85–88
  of teachers, to program, 78, 80, 81–82
Adjunct course, 30, 34
Administration, of IEPs, 3
  decisions in, student feedback and, 143
  participatory, 136
  principles of excellence in, 82–83, 88
  support for reflective teaching, 144
Advanced levels
  credit for courses at, 110, 111
  university-link activities at, 27*f*, 29–31
Advisors, IEP, 2
  in Graduate Research and Writing (GRW)
     course, 43–44
  for learning disabled students, 125
AED. *See* Academy for Educational
  Development
Affective factors, in IEP curriculum, 23–24

American Association of Intensive English
  Programs (AAIEP), 1, 110, 135
American University (AU), ELI at, 123
  Learning Skills Program of, 125–130
  practical ideas from, 130–133
  student body of, 123
Anonymity, in course evaluations, 137
Apprenticeship of observation, 85
Arizona. *See* Northern Arizona University
Assessment
  clear points for, 101
  of content-integrated-skills-based
     approach (CISB), 19–20
  course. *See* Course evaluations
  designing measures for, 60
  in IEPs, 3
  in TESOL courses, 69, 72
Association of International Educators
  (NAFSA), 1
At-risk learners. *See* Learning disabilities
Attendance, monitoring, 128
Australia. *See* Monash University
Authentic language, integrating into
  curriculum, 18

B

Bailey, K. M., 72
Baker, E. D., 65, 67, 73, 75
Barnhardt, S., 32
Bartlett, L., 136
Beaubien, R., 133
Beebe, L. M., 86
Beginning levels
  instructional focus at, 38–39
  university-link activities at, 26, 27*f*, 31
Benesch, S., 3

Also Available From TESOL

Academic Writing Programs
Ilona Leki, Editor

Action Research
Julian Edge, Editor

Bilingual Education
Donna Christian and Fred Genesee, Editors

CALL Environments:
Research, Practice, and Critical Issues
Joy Egbert and Elizabeth Hanson-Smith, Editors

Distance-Learning Programs
Lynn E. Henrichsen, Editor

Implementing the ESL Standards for Pre-K–12 Students Through Teacher Education
Marguerite Ann Snow, Editor

Integrating the ESL Standards Into Classroom Practice: Grades Pre-K–2
Betty Ansin Smallwood, Editor

Integrating the ESL Standards Into Classroom Practice: Grades 3–5
Katharine Davies Samway, Editor

Integrating the ESL Standards Into Classroom Practice: Grades 6–8
Suzanne Irujo, Editor

Integrating the ESL Standards Into Classroom Practice: Grades 9–12
Barbara Agor, Editor

Internet for English Teaching
Mark Warschauer, Heidi Shetzer, and Christine Meloni

Journal Writing
Jill Burton and Michael Carroll, Editors

Reading and Writing in More Than One Language:
Lessons for Teachers
Elizabeth Franklin, Editor

Teacher Education
Karen E. Johnson, Editor

Teaching in Action: Case Studies From Second Language Classrooms
Jack C. Richards, Editor

Technology-Enhanced Learning Environments
Elizabeth Hanson-Smith, Editor

For more information, contact
Teachers of English to Speakers of Other Languages, Inc.
700 South Washington Street, Suite 200
Alexandria, Virginia 22314 USA
Tel 703-836-0774 • Fax 703-836-6447 • publications@tesol.org •
http://www.tesol.org/